To The Students, Faculty, and Administration of Lincoln Memorial University, who honor the contribution of Dr. Preston Bradley

January 1, 1973

Sincerely,
Daniel Rose Chandler

DANIEL ROSS CHANDLER was born in Lincoln County, Oklahoma, in 1937. He was awarded a B.S. in Speech Education from Oklahoma University; an M.A. in Speech-English from Purdue University; a B.D. in Religion from Garrett Theological Seminary at Northwestern University; and a Ph.D. in Communication from Ohio University. He studied at the University of Chicago and the University of Southern California. He has published numerous scholarly and popular articles and compiled and edited Dr. Bradley's recent book, *Between You and Me*.

Dr. Chandler served as the Assistant Pastor of the Peoples Church of Chicago and Dr. Preston Bradley's understudy. Recently he served as an Auburn Resident Pastor, Union Theological Seminary, New York City, and studied at Yale University. In September he joins the faculty of the Bernard M. Baruch College, the City University of New York.

THE REVEREND DR. PRESTON BRADLEY

The Official, Authorized Biography of

THE REVEREND DR. PRESTON BRADLEY

by
Daniel Ross Chandler

Exposition Press   New York

BR1725
B68
C48

EXPOSITION PRESS INC.

50 Jericho Turnpike   Jericho, New York 11753

FIRST EDITION

© 1971 by Daniel Ross Chandler *All rights reserved, including the right of reproduction in whole or in part in any form except for short quotations in critical essays and reviews.* Manufactured in the United States of America.

LIBRARY OF CONGRESS CATALOG CARD NUMBER: 78-166186

0-682-47333-2

To My Families

North of Chandler and in Chicago

CONTENTS

PREFACE 9
INTRODUCTION 13

PART ONE: *A Biography*

I.	*Boyhood Beginnings*	25
II.	*Early Speech Training*	27
III.	*The Early Chicago Ministry*	31
IV.	*Public Tributes and Family Occasions*	38
V.	*Rebirth of the Peoples Church of Chicago*	40
VI.	*Preaching*	44
VII.	*The Broadcasting Ministry*	45
VIII.	*Author and Critic*	48
IX.	*Highlights Along the Way*	50
X.	*Dimensions of Ministry*	51
XI.	*Involvement in the Life of His Time*	56
XII.	*Near the End of a Career*	61
XIII.	*Toward a Common Humanity*	66
XIV.	*Arden*	69

PART TWO:
Sermons by the Reverend Dr. Preston Bradley

What Is Christianity?	73
Do We Need Another Reformation?	77
Is God Dead?	81
Space-Age Religion	85
The Celebration of Life	89
They Call It Progress	92
Red or Dead?	96
I Believe	101
If I Had Only One Sermon to Preach	104

NOTES 109
BIBLIOGRAPHY 117

PREFACE

The three o'clock afternoon appointment on May 25, 1964, began when I sat in the living room of Dr. Preston Bradley's apartment home on Lakeview Avenue, Chicago. Suddenly the door opened, a shaft of light illumined a darkened hallway, and a beaming pastor resembling an Irish leprechaun entered. Returning from a busy afternoon of ministerial engagements, Dr. Bradley invited me into his book-lined study and offered me an appointment as his assistant. He moved me deeply.

Later, standing outside his apartment waiting for the elevator, we talked together. Knowing that the closing elevator doors would eventually block the view between us, I slipped my fingers between the doors to prevent them from closing. Some emotion passed between us. Nothing verbally was spoken, but there was an emotional experience.

The same sensation was present the last time I visited him before leaving to complete my doctorate. A gleam from his eyes, a warmth from his face, a quietness in a whispered farewell contained a simple eloquence which he described in his book *Between You and Me;* "The loveliest remembrance of parting is most frequently that unpremeditated and spontaneous gesture of goodby that comes when words can no longer be heard. That last goodby that speaks the language of the soul does not need the physical utterance to portray the depth and beauty of its spirit." The prominent pastor taught me that love is greater than eloquence, although love provides the incentive and inspiration which prompts some men to speak.

The remembrances which are treasured from my days at the Peoples Church grow more brilliant through the years. There were times, when the congregation had departed and the lights were dim, that I returned to the auditorium, sat upon the platform steps, glanced across the circular rows of vacant seats, and wondered about the future of the church. One specific event remains memorable. One night I worked late, growing very tired. So I went back into the vestry, removed cushions from the furniture, laid them across the floor, and slept upon that improvised bed. The church is situated close to restless, surging Lake Michigan. And during the early morning hours the temperature fell. I was cold, very cold. So I went to the closet, took out a robe, covered myself with it, and finished my night's sleep. I am amused recalling sleeping a few feet from an historic, world-famous pulpit. Strange how memories rest in our minds and hearts until something triggers them into consciousness.

My respect for Dr. Bradley remains constant. From personal experiences with the everyday problems, passions, and perplexities human beings encounter, he developed a religious philosophy which sustains his ministry. Although he serves countless persons congested beneath metropolitan skyscrapers and tenement-infested Lawrence Avenue highrises, his ministry stretches beyond the run-down dilapidated surroundings and encircles the globe. An unorthodox Presbyterian who withdrew from the Chicago presbytery as an inclusive religious liberal, he maintains a religious nonconformity and spiritual sensitivity. Deeply involved in the quiet struggles, the desperate anxieties, and painful sacrifices of humans enduring life's demanding realities, unsupported by ecclesiastical assistance from denominational institutions or sectarian associations, he sustains a mighty ministry. Compassionate before human need and human nature, he responds to agony that is so deep that sometimes the suffering cannot speak; he vicariously participates in the broken hopes, the heartaches, and the human tragedies of persons. And from his service to humanity grew the largest nonsectarian and nondenominational congregations in the world, one of the longest known tenures in an American pulpit, and the oldest continuous radio religious broadcast in the United States.

No one characteristic explains his ministry, but a statement he made on one occasion, the funeral elegy of his pastor, the Reverend Dr. Morriston J. Thomas, reflects the reverence for life he has which pervades his service. Dr. Bradley stated: "God honored me by giving me life as he honored you—we've all been honored to have known life. I know of no religion higher than honoring the life God gives us." Committed to that intellectual integrity which never replaces personal thinking with bland conformity to a theological dogma or an ecclesiastical ceremony, he manifests a courageous confidence although he stands alone and speaks for a religious minority.

Never equating corporate bigness with human greatness, conscious that life's major influences are silent and unseen, he has earned that living immortality he described. When speaking on January 23, 1966, he stated in "If I Had Only One Sermon to Preach," what might summarize his ministry: "I want it to be said of me after I am gone and the last sermon has been preached and the last experience of life has been lived—I would rather have written upon any remnant that I leave this sentence, than any other: 'He tried to be a friend of all mankind.' " The Reverend Dr. Preston Bradley is a friend of humanity.

DANIEL ROSS CHANDLER

The College of Communication
The Interpersonal Communication School
Ohio University
Athens, Ohio
July 22, 1970

INTRODUCTION

No matter how accustomed one might happen to be to speaking and writing, there come times when one feels almost speechless. One is so dominated by many associations which are not primarily a part of a communication activity that it becomes difficult to correlate one's thoughts and formulate them into language.

It is one of these occasions that I find myself facing when reflecting upon nearly sixty years in a single pulpit. When I look back over these years, I see that I have given almost 150 public addresses each year, which, when viewed as a whole, seems like a lot of talk, and when gathered together, makes an avalanche of written and spoken language.

For nearly sixty years it has been my great privilege—and I desire every friend and member of this church to recognize that I emphasize the word *privilege*—to stand in this pulpit and speak to the most responsive group of men and women to be found anywhere in the world. And yet, during all this period I have never entered the pulpit once without fear and trembling. Every once in a while there are those who come to me and say: "You seem to have so much confidence and so much control with those audiences when we hear you. You do it as though it were easy and not difficult. How do you do it?" If they only knew what I know and what I would have each of you know in this intimate, personal introduction to a book commemorating and celebrating my ministry at the Peoples Church of Chicago. I have never overcome, and I am quite certain now, after nearly a century of living, that I shall never overcome, the nervousness and timidity that precedes every sermon and address I deliver in public and every statement I write for publication. There are those of you who might think that the occasion always belies that fact; but the fact of the matter is that just before every occasion of significance

—such as the significance of writing this message—I am dominated by an anxiety and a restlessness which is unexplainable to me.

It is awesome to me that I am looking across a very long ministry and many years of my life. I wish that I had twenty-five years left. The sermons are mostly all preached, and the books are nearly finished. But I would like to live through the next quarter of a century. I know that I am writing to a vast number of men and women who, in this hectic, nervous age of transition and experimentation, are anxiously hoping that something will be said that will make a contribution to their individual problems and social adjustments. I have so much in my heart that I would like to say today, and probably much of it is of such an intimate character that it ought not to be said at all. But I could not serve a people for nearly half a century without developing relationships that are so beautiful and fragile that at every opportunity I desire that they may be enriched in their loveliness and that I meet the responsibilities demanded.

I have never lost faith in this pulpit. And notwithstanding the constant association of the years, I have felt that every Sunday morning, every Sunday night, and every Wednesday night was a direct challenge that you brought to me. I could not rest on the past, and I could not fail to realize that in a city of discriminating character where the opportunity for information and accessibility of fact is so universal for all people, anyone who dares assume to speak or write or preach must be continuously alert and keep the capacity of yonder-mindedness. The moment a member of my church or a listener on the air anticipates me in an attitude of thought, or an interpretation of philosophy, or familiarity with a great book, or kinship with great music or art, the moment I fail in yonder-mindedness, I fail in everything else. Consequently, when you stand alone, as I have stood in an unorthodox, free pulpit, without support and encouragement of the great national denominations with their fabulous wealth and their organizational strength, I have to face this challenge—your challenge—daily and weekly all these years.

I discovered that the church statistics of the city of Chicago

Introduction 15

reveal that the average pastorate of a clergyman in a Chicago pulpit, over a period of twenty-five years' observation, is only seven years, and that the average clergyman in a Chicago pulpit is worn out, rusts out, or fades out in some way among the active ministry in our city. Seven years of constant anxiety, seven years of challenge is the limit; and I think of these years and then think of how I tried to keep my mind focused in the tomorrow and not become devitalized by the traditions of the past.

I have been a part of the changing order and the fluctuating moods of civilization, having seen the epochs bring their psychological rebounds to the temper of my people, having experienced the thrill of days of prosperity when your contributions and your spirits felt the flush and the ease of victory, having passed with you during these years through the awful psychosis of international hate that expressed itself in the bitter brutality of that useless institution called war, having passed with you through the various changes that came to the thinking modes of the best civilization on the great fundamental problems involved in religious philosophy, having shared with you the joys of your fireside and stood beside you and shared the agony of your tears. I have given your youngsters names, I have married you, I have stood beside you when the black angel broke the unity of your fireside, I have wept with you beside an open grave, I have listened to your confessions, and I have shared with you the remorse for our mutual sins. Life has placed us together. We have attempted during every one of the years to do the best that we could; and it is in moments of retrospection that one realizes how much one has failed.

My ministry, in its early years, was a lonely one. I came to Chicago unknown and unwelcomed. I came here in all of the enthusiasm of youth, hoping to add to an inadequate education. I had sought and hoped that perhaps my place in life could ultimately find expression in some of the great communions of religion; but by a nature and temperament for which I am not responsible, I have never been able to accept religion in terms of tradition. Man-made creeds never stirred me. Orthodox ideas of heaven and hell always revolted me. An anthropomorphic idea of an elongated personality created out of the will and life-wish of humanity into the term *God* never answered the intellectual idea, and what is still more, the moral idea, of what I thought God must be. And, of course, that alienated me from any association whatsoever with orthodox religion. I had to be an outcast and a rebel. Ecclesiastical hierarchy, Catholic, Protestant or Jewish, shuddered at that which I conceived religion at its best might be for the world. So those early years were not always smooth for me. I was rather intolerant and not a little dogmatic. I thought that perhaps my intolerance and dogmatism were a part of my youth, until I lived long enough to know other people who are older who have not lost the ability to be equally intolerant and dogmatic. It would seem, then, that dogmatism and intolerance cannot be definitely attributed as one of the failures and one of the obstacles of being young.

But I wanted a religion that could be answered by reason. I did not want a religion, or a belief about religion, that was incredulous, that approached a direct attack upon my intelligence. I wanted a religion that was intelligent. Miracles never interested me, because I never made it an issue that God had to be a circus performer and violate His own laws to be convincing that He was all-powerful. The violation of nature's laws to demonstrate the capacity of God always was repugnant to me and is now. Consequently, you can readily understand that I was further alienated from an orthodox interpretation of religion. It made me very lonely and very unhappy, but I demanded of whatever conception of God which would be possible for me to encompass that He must be, at any rate, as good and as fine as my own blessed father. I could never visualize a God that could look down upon parched fields, suffering dumb brutes, and the destruction of crops and famine—a God who would see all that and then wait until a man groveled on his knees and prayed for rain would be a God that was not worth praying to. My Father would not do that! My human father would not do that! You would not do it, and God would not do it! And so, I wanted a character in my interpretation of God that would give me a moral God, a God that was moral and not a God that had to be worshipped, not a God that had to say: "I am a jealous and an envious God, I am the Lord

God Jehovah!" I didn't want a tribal God, or a racial God; I wanted a God of Love! You don't have to get Love to do the things that Love can do. Love is spontaneous! Love is sacrificial! Love is creative, and GOD IS LOVE!

So that made those early years years of great loneliness, years that I think of today as pioneer years. What I mean by that in this confession of years of struggle with a free pulpit and people, is that other people have come into this city and have entered great, beautiful churches, Gothic halls, Gothic aisles, rose windows stained and made beautiful by sunlight through color, old churches, churches where membership meant social security and a certain element of respectability, churches where it was the proper thing to belong, churches that were safe, churches that were secure. Ministers coming to them and accepting the situation had ease and comfort—something I never knew, my friends, and never had.

In the first congregation in this city I had sixty-eight people. I was living in a room for which I paid $2.00 a week, and my salary was what was left after the expenses for the Sunday service were paid, which sometimes—most times—was rather slim. In those far-off days, and I know you will forgive me for being reminiscent—who could be anything but reminiscent—in those far-off days four motifs dominated my ministry.

The first motif was seeing if I could give to humankind a sensitivity to the realities of religion that was not circumscribed by creed or church. That was my motif years ago. That's the motif for which I have had to suffer, and that's the motif for which I have been criticized, merely because the dominant theme of my life is that humanity has a potentiality which, if properly disciplined by intellectual understanding and saturated by a desire to help their fellows, could build a world of peace and happiness for everybody. That has been my thesis. And wherever I have seen religion express itself in terms of a locativeness that shut me out, there was something about it that was not true. When a church closes its door in the face of an individual merely because he does not accept the entire thesis of the orthodox religion, then I know there is something about that church that is not true. When any church says: "I am the only true church; mine is the only true creed," no matter what that church is, or how old it is, that church is wrong. For no church was ever established and no creed was ever written that was big enough to contain all the truth of the divine God, the Father of all mankind. No church has a mortgage on truth. No bishop, no minister, no rabbi has any more right in the eyes of the pilgrim souls trying to find the truth of life than any other. I believe in the priesthood of the laity. Every individual heart trying to find its adjustment and answer to its problems can feel the thrill of triumph. You are the priest, and you are the minister, and you are the rabbi. For the church is one province and one union. It does not make any difference what your color is, or whether you are Catholic, Protestant or Jewish. It is the universal church that dominates today.

The second motif that has dominated my ministry is the recognition of the potentiality of human nature to be something better than it is. Believing in brotherhood of man with all my heart and strength—there is the cornerstone of my church! Not the sacrament, not how you shall be baptized. It makes no difference whether you sprinkle, dip, or pour. I am not interested at all in any theological program. I am much more concerned about getting it in the hearts of mankind that every individual is a part of the divine. It is not so much that I believe in the divinity of one man as that I believe in the divinity of all men. Mankind is divine; and every heart is a child of God, an heir of the eternal. It is your divinity that inspires me.

The third motif that has characterized my ministry all these years is a thing that has made for me more enemies than either of the other two, and one of the favorite pastimes of people who don't know is to say that Dr. Bradley is an atheist! I hear that every now and then.

And finally, the fourth motif reflects my social, economic, and industrial attitude. I am not concerned with what happens to me after I am dead, or what happens to you. I believe that whatever happens to me after I am dead, or to you, will not depend very largely upon what church you attended, what creed you bowed to, or whether you followed the dictates of an assimilated religion. On the contrary, I think that what counts is the immortality of achievement, and here and now I am building mansions or hovels for my soul. So are you. I am going to have a kind of eternity that I am creating now. I am not *going into* eternity; I am *already in it*. Death is only an incident and not nearly as important as people think it is. I am building my mansions, or I am hammering out my hovels. I am painting my pictures; in that long, long night of the unknown, I shall walk up and down the gallery that I have painted, and it shall be my heaven or my hell. The brush is made of earth; the paint is made of earth. It was given to me here, and the canvas is my life.

That is the religion I believe in, because I look out into a world selfish and greedy; where youth is made into cannon fodder and good things are burned and scattered; where there are ugliness and battlefields, depression and panic settling down upon them; where there are injustice and poverty; where the few revel with too much while the poor are suffering with too little. That religion, when it sensitizes our souls, would inspire us to do something for a world like this. And that has been my religion and will be, if I am privileged, for years more.

The last thought is this. I look back on every one of those years with gratitude. I am glad I could pioneer. I am glad I did not have anybody to lean on. I am glad there was no denomination to protect me. I am glad that I did not have a church that was bowed down under the urge of respectability and the essence of safety. I am glad that our doors have been open to both rich and poor. I am glad that Jew, Gentile, and Catholic are welcome here. This is almost the only pulpit and place in four and a half million people where we don't have a thesis that is dependent upon our own selfish interests. The days have been long, the nights have been difficult, and the world has been tempestuous.

The only little pang I feel in my heart is a sense of my failures. I have failed so many of you. You came to me with your broken hearts, and I could not heal them. Some were in great difficulty, and there was nothing I could do. I failed you, and you have felt it deeply. That's a tragic experience for a pastor to feel. I could not do more than I tried to do. But I know how much some of you needed me and how, if I could have multiplied myself into five other men, I could not have done it. Won't you forgive me for the failure if you have leaned on me and I have disappointed you? You have come to me for jobs, and I had none. You have come to me with your financial disasters, and I had no money. You have come to me with your family troubles and tears, and I have not always been able to bring you harmony. Won't you feel that my work, in this sense of failure, was certainly a failure of the head and not the heart and the will? Please feel that if it were up to me, every jobless person in the world would be working tomorrow; every burdened heart would have its burden lifted. If I could! IF I COULD, I would do it!

So when you expect me to be something that I am not, just cover my defects, will you, with a mantle of charity. And if you feel I have failed you, please remember the kind of a failure it was, will you? If in some way I have made the road a little easier for some of you who have come into worship some Sunday morning low spirited and down at the heels and have gone out with your head a little higher and with a lighter heart, I am glad. The world will get out of its trouble.

The thing of my ministry that I never doubted, I believe with all my mind and heart and soul, is the inevitable law of progress. The world is going on; and it is going forward; and there is no man and no group of nations that can stop it. *Man is going to win in the battles of tomorrow.* So I still have my dreams, and I am still keeping my hopes, and I am holding onto my ideals; and with these inviolate, I plan to continue my ministry so long as I am able, determined that when the history of my ministry is written and the volume published, its message will emphasize the brotherhood of man, the Fatherhood of God, the leadership of Jesus, and human progress.

During my ministry, Dr. Chandler served the Peoples Church and me as the Assistant Pastor and Minister of Youth. I am grateful beyond words that he has written a comprehensive and definitive history of my ministry in our beloved church. With a generous and gracious grant from the W. Clement and Jessie V. Stone Foundation, he served our congregation, accompanying me in the pulpit during the Sunday worship services, traveling with me on speaking engagements, writing for the church magazine, studying my private papers and personal manuscripts, and conducting research for his doctoral dissertation. I cherish his friendship and wish him a great future.

PRESTON BRADLEY

Senior Pastor
The Peoples Church of Chicago
July 21, 1970

PART ONE
A Biography

I. Boyhood Beginnings

Preston Bradley was born to Robert McFarlan Bradley and Anna Elizabeth Warren Bradley on August 18, 1888, in Linden, Michigan. Robert Bradley immigrated from the county of Antrim, in northern Ireland, and served Linden as the village blacksmith. Anna Bradley was a farmer's daughter and the village seamstress. She never attended school after she reached fourteen. Robert left school when he was fifteen. Three years after Preston's birth, his sister Beulah was born, extending the closely knit family circle.

Preston Bradley spent his boyhood surrounded by diverse religious elements. The Bradleys were Irish Presbyterians who attended the village Presbyterian church, where the blacksmith once served as the session clerk. Within this population of five hundred residents were three competing churches and two rival sects. The fundamentalist Free Methodist Church was described in *Courage for Today:*

> Near my uncle's farm stood a little white wooden structure known as the Free Methodist Church. That denomination is intensely Fundamentalist, and often shows its enthusiasm by screaming, clapping of hands, jerking and jumping, choking and the like. When I was a boy my aunt belonged to this church. At every opportunity I went with her, for I was fascinated by the country preachers, with their vivid, vital and strong-voiced theology.[1]

Although the youthful Preston attended the Presbyterian Sunday school when he was four years old and was baptized in the Presbyterian Church, he occasionally attended the Free Methodist Church. He described the typical Linden minister's mentality when he preached "The Atheist Nobody Knows" on December 4, 1927:

> Some of the ministers of our churches in the little village could not recognize an idea if someone had embossed it upon a lovely card and presented it to them; they were utterly incapable of appreciating the potentialities of the human mind, the resourcefulness of the human mind, and the capacity of the human mind to penetrate into the universe and to discover there what it is all about.[2]

Nevertheless, Preston Bradley stated in *Mastering Fear:* "I sat in a little white church and swallowed what the minister said hook, line and sinker."[3] He also cherished a copy of Phillips Brooks' *Lectures on Preaching,* which his parents gave him, and *The Life of Dwight L. Moody,* presented to him during a Sunday school convention. Concerning the evangelist Moody, Preston Bradley stated in his autobiographical *Along the Way:* "Undoubtedly, his career was a factor in causing me to choose Chicago as the scene of my career, instead of, say, Detroit."[4]

Although many persons around the boy were conservative fundamentalists, Preston Bradley was stimulated mentally by the Linden agnostic, Dr. H. H. Case. Dr. Case's efforts to enlarge the youth's imagination and intelligence were discussed in a Sunday morning sermon:

> Now, Dr. Case was called an atheist! I can remember well hearing our preacher stand in our pulpit in the little white church beside the maple-covered road in the little village, and raising his voice in vehement denunciation against those "in our midst" who believed there was no God. Now, the fact of the matter was my atheist never said he believed there was no God. . . .
> He was the type of scientist that utilized every bit of information concerning the universe in which he lived, and molded it into a relationship with himself which did not need nor ask for teachers or prophet, but who accepted the universe in the terms in which he found it.[5]

Surrounded by pervasive fundamentalism, Dr. Case confronted Preston Bradley with an appreciation of freedom of inquiry, tolerance of diverse beliefs, and the importance of scientific investigation.

The beauty of field and stream with which nature blessed

Linden provided a source for recreation and education. The Shiawassee River, running through the lake-fringed hamlet, provided a swimming hole on humid summer days. Rowing a boat on nearby Loon Lake was physical exercise for a growing boy. Downstream the twisted branches of an oak tree sprawled above Preston's favorite swimming hole. Behind his boyhood home stood a gristmill. Before the construction of cement, asphalt, and graveled highways, Preston's transportation included the squeaking, jerking, and lunging horse-drawn buggy.

During his boyhood young Preston sold newspapers, worked in his father's blacksmith shop, and studied the writings of Shakespeare and Emerson. His early interest in public speaking is evidenced by his winning a county-wide speech contest in 1905 eulogizing Theodore Roosevelt; and as a high school senior, "the boy orator of the Shiawassee" won the Michigan public speaking championship.[6] Following high school graduation, he became a printer's devil with the *Linden Leader,* worked with a Washington hand press, and published his "Thought Seeds" column with the editor's encouragement.[7]

II. *Early Speech Training*

Familiar with the heritage and traditions of American public address, Preston Bradley developed his interest in rhetoric early in life and shared a personal friendship with several of America's most famous spokesmen. In *Along the Way* he recalled that "preaching or at least speaking was so fascinating to me, even before I was ten, that I would go out into the back yard of my home and launch into what I considered to be an oration."[8] The Michigan youth who delivered his first speech before the Linden High School Parliamentary Society[9] made his dramatic debut playing Mark Antony in a high school theatrical production of Shakespeare's *Julius Caesar.*[10] When Dr. Bradley preached "The Living Shakespeare" on April 23, 1939, he recalled

> ... the day when I played Shakespeare. I made my debut in public in a Shakespearean role. I was fifteen years old, a student in high school, and I played Mark Antony in the play of *Julius Caesar*. My costume was the Woodmans' robe. We had a Woodsman's lodge in our little town and we figured how we could possibly get any costumes to play Shakespeare. All I needed was just a robe, and I remember my entrance with horror, and my exit with joy, when, in a robe that was much too long for me, and sleeves that were also much too long, I stood in front of the teacher's desk with the others in the parts about me, with a lot of grinning folks in my audience, while with all of the dignity and charm of a Shakespearean barnstormer I read Mark Antony's great speech upon the death of Julius Caesar.[11]

During his boyhood, Preston Bradley was significantly impressed by several public speakers whose rhetoric arrested his attention. A *Chicago's American* newspaper article reports that incentive came when his parents insisted that the family attend a lecture in Linden given by an Iowa minister, Dr. Henry Clark. The youthful Preston sat enthralled in the front row. When the speaker finished, Mrs. Bradley whispered to her son that her happiest moment would be hearing Preston delivering a speech. That night, in his back yard before a stone pile which Preston considered his audience, he delivered his first speech.[12]

He gained speaking experience in the Linden graveyard. A marble tombstone about four feet high held an open marble book, above which Preston's head barely showed. The boy and his younger sister summoned their friends to the cemetery, where Preston bade them sit upon the surrounding graves. From behind the tombstone, young Preston conducted church services and preached to the assembled company. He later remembered: "I have definite recollections of having difficulty in maintaining respectful decorum and I was a little severe. Sometimes the church service would end up in a good row, but I loved it and I never could get away from the appeal of the preacher."[13]

Through high school, his favorite activity was public speaking. He took every opportunity to hear lectures by Chautauqua or lyceum speakers who visited Linden, Argentine, Fenton, and

Early Speech Training

Clio.[14] William Jennings Bryan was in his prime during Preston Bradley's boyhood, and hearing Bryan in the Detroit Armory was a memorable highlight from the 1900 political campaign.

> Even now as I write these lines, the emotions of that experience are undimmed by the passing of sixty years. Imagination, that most necessary faculty for all creative work, was lavished with her favours. . . . I turned my face to the right and I saw Bryan striding down the spacious aisle.
> His face was wreathed in smiles and illuminated by his ever-present geniality. The irresistible and irrepressible Bryan! The man with a thousand charms; a man who, as an individual, exerted a greater personal influence than any of his contemporaries.[15]

In *Courage for Today* Dr. Bradley recalled: "One of my boyhood longings was to have lived at a time when I could hear Daniel Webster make a speech."[16] His interest in Abraham Lincoln seems evident:

> Of Abraham Lincoln I read all I could find. He is probably the greatest figure that America has produced, if we have to choose one person. For what he has come to represent in humanity, tolerance, and compassion, Lincoln may be the greatest figure that the Western world has produced.[17]

Not only did Dr. Bradley later travel on the Chautauqua circuit with William Jennings Bryan, but also he knew the prominent Chicago criminal lawyer with whom Bryan debated during the historic religious controversy known as the Scopes Trial.

> I knew Darrow for more than thirty-five years before his death in 1938. I shared several platforms with him. One memorable occasion was at Sinai Temple in 1932, when Darrow talked on law, Scott Nearing on economics, Dr. Mann on social planning, and I on religion.
> I debated with Darrow twice, once at the Peoples Church and another time at the Garrick Theatre.[18]

While busts of Abraham Lincoln and Ralph Waldo Emerson adorned the chancel of the Peoples Church of Chicago, Dr. Bradley sometimes mentioned another prominent platform personality in glowing eulogy. When the unconventional clergyman delivered "The Atheist Nobody Knows" on December 4, 1927, he said: "I remember as a boy when the words 'Robert G. Ingersoll' to me just brought visions of a devil and sense of hell, until it seemed I could feel the sulphur flames in the pressure of that orthodox emphasis of my far-off childhood."[19] When Dr. Bradley preached "Where Is God Now?" on January 11, 1942, he defended Ingersoll's unorthodoxy by contending: "The mind of Ingersoll was a mind that raised itself in attack against the superstition and bigotry of the religion of his day."[20] From personal acquaintance or studying history, Preston Bradley possessed an intimate familiarity with famous American speakers such as William Jennings Bryan, Daniel Webster, Abraham Lincoln, Clarence Darrow, and Robert G. Ingersoll.

Preston Bradley attended a small Presbyterian liberal arts college, Alma College, in Alma, Michigan, during the 1905-1906 academic year. In *Along the Way* he described his first night at Alma College:

> The first evening at Alma went along pretty well for me until it came time to go to bed. Then I opened my suitcase and saw, resting on top of my homemade shirts and homemade bathrobe, something Father and Mother knew I loved—a great big, beautiful, colorful Michigan apple! I sat down with tears running down my face.[21]

During freshman orientation at Alma College, Preston became deeply moved when convocation speaker, the Reverend William A. Quayle from St. James Methodist Church in Chicago, challenged his audience: "Follow the gleam, young man! Follow the gleam!"[22] With this inspiration and encouragement, Preston worked his way through his freshman year by tending a doctor's team of horses, waiting upon tables, and preaching. Continuing his preaching as a college undergraduate, he ministered in Hillman, Montmorency County, Michigan. Eventually he served three pastorates within the county. Preston preached at Port Hope, and he served in Grand Blanc between 1907 and 1909.

Speaking in secular situations, Preston Bradley accepted his first professional lecture engagement on May 22, 1907, when he addressed an organization called "Phun, Philosophy and Phoolishness" at a meeting in Benton Harbor. Indicating an interest in journalism, Preston sold an article to the *True American and Rural Advocate,* a newspaper published by a Battle Creek Presbyterian clergyman, Dr. W. A. Taylor. Beginning in January, 1907, Preston served briefly as an advertising manager for that newspaper.

He read law in Flint, Michigan, between 1906 and 1909, studied as a special student at the University of Michigan during the academic year 1909-1910, and finally completed his Doctor of Civil Law degree at the Hamilton College of Law in Chicago in 1915.

III. *The Early Chicago Ministry*

In 1911 Preston Bradley arrived in Chicago with twenty-eight cents, secured housing in the home of Mrs. Annie Bates at 3733 Ogden Avenue, and studied at the Moody Bible Institute. Although Moody Institute was instrumental in furthering his education, he was suspended for committing several "sins," like smoking a pipe and attending the theater.[23]

The Reverend Dr. Preston Bradley ministered as student-pastor of a small Chicago Presbyterian congregation, the Church of Providence, in 1912. But when he renounced the Westminster Confession's categorical damnation of unbaptized infants during a sermon, Dr. Bradley was asked by the presbytery to reconsider his theological position or cease considering the Presbyterian ministry. He admitted the heresy charges, withdrew from the presbytery, and served as minister to eighty-six[24] persons who followed him. *Newsweek* gave the following explanation on October 1, 1962:

> DAMNED: Fresh out of the University of Michigan and into a Presbyterian pulpit in Chicago, Bradley quickly landed in

trouble with church conservatives by contending that formal baptism was not necessary to find grace before God. "If God was a God who damned children for not being baptized," explains Bradley, "then I couldn't accept Him. I said it then and I say it now."

Saying it then was enough to make him split with the Presbyterians, although most of his iconoclastic ideas he had 50 years ago are accepted by most Protestant denominations today. He then became pastor of the Peoples Church, which had been founded by a liberal Methodist.[25]

Having served the Church of Providence in Chicago between 1911 and 1912, Dr. Bradley resigned his ministerial affiliation on July 1, 1912.

> In any event to go back, I was not put on trial for heresy; they did not have to try me. I admitted the charge. I simply resigned from Presbyterianism. Fortunately for me, eighty-six of the 100 members of my church resigned right along with me.[26]

Connie Meyers explained in the *Chicago's American* on October 15, 1967:

> Brought up in a strict Calvinist tradition, Dr. Bradley broke with the Presbyterian faith in 1912 and founded the Peoples Church "because I couldn't accept the belief that God would send an unbaptized infant to Hell."[27]

Dr. Bradley conducted the first worship service for an independent church when sixty-eight persons congregated in a small hall in Viking Temple on July 7, 1912. He described the situation as follows:

> We were a small group of people who had a deep faith in the future of our liberal and free church. Not one person present had any traditions of liberality in religious thought or organization. We had all stepped boldly out of ecclesiastical bondage and theological servitude.[28]

During the following week, a group assembled in Mr. and Mrs. William H. Purse's home on Walton Avenue and established the Peoples Progressive Church of Chicago. Within five years the name was changed. For a month the new congregation assembled in Viking Temple; then they moved to Arcola Hall at Clark and Addison. Mrs. Philip E. Gould and Mr. William Hickock, two members from the group inaugurated by Dr. Hiram W. Thomas, visited Bradley's church and proposed that the two congregations combine. When this invitation was accepted the church experienced substantial growth.[29]

While Dr. Bradley traveled Chautauqua and lyceum routes, growing numbers followed the minister's leadership. During the fall of 1913 the congregation moved into a very large theater outside Chicago's Loop, the Wilson Avenue Theater. The "silver-tongued orator of the Shiawassee" reigned eloquent.

> He calls himself a Sociologist. His love of humanity has made him this and he is not in the same class with the ordinary lecturer. A pronounced individuality sends him along other intellectual routes. His messages are filled with dashes of humor, beautiful figures and nuggets of philosophy. No mannerisms handicap him, and his humanitarian spirit, his sympathy for the underdog and his exemplification of the Great Life leaves a mighty impression.[30]

Speaking at Chautauqua meetings and ministering to the Wilson Avenue Theater congregation, the lyceum lecturer preached excessively about God instead of Emerson, relying upon the Bible and praising Jesus.[31] In 1918 the congregation convened in the magnificent Pantheon Theater on Sheridan Road, a beautiful auditorium seating three thousand. The *Lyceum News*, published by the Redpath Vawter management in Cedar Rapids, Iowa, described the lecturer this way:

> Dr. Preston Bradley, pastor of the Peoples Church, Chicago, appeared at Grand Junction, Iowa, December 9, one of the coldest and stormiest nights of the winter, and did not have a very large audience, but from the extended "first page, top of column" write-up given to him by the *Globe,* he evidently made good. That newspaper says:
> "To make a long story short this one number was well worth the price of admission. We have heard Bryan speak to a packed audience when everything was to his advantage and we say it truthfully that Wm. J. Bryan has 'nothing over on' Dr. Bradley.

He is a real orator and not a second-rater at that. For two full hours he held his audience spellbound and then they were eager for him to continue—none but a real orator and one who has a message can pull such a trick with a small audience on a miserable night."[32]

The sensation the Reverend Dr. Bradley created there seems comparable to this response from an Englishman describing the Chicago clergyman preaching in the Pantheon:

> And at first, taking in these details, while the choir sang for us, I thought the whole affair rather irreligious, its atmosphere one of mere showmanship, if you understand what I mean.
> But the moment the choir ceased singing, and Bradley, after the shortest of prayers, rose up and spoke with us, all criticism became impossible to my spellbound mind. For here was fire; here was passion; here was the brain of a profound thinker—and oratory—oratory such as we hardly ever hear in England, even "the gift of tongues."[33]

When Dr. Bradley became senior pastor, newspaperman Leonard Dubkin remembered encountering the popular pastor during the clergyman's early ministry.

> I have known Dr. Bradley for about 30 years. I first met him when he delivered a lecture at the Monte Randall Forum, for which I was the public relations man. This was a forum in which we asked famous people to speak.
> After his talk a lot of wild radicals got up and virtually tore him to pieces. The audience enjoyed it tremendously.
> I had talked to him before the forum and wanted him to be prepared to be torn apart. "Oh, I'm not afraid," he said. "Greater men than I have been afraid."
> I thought his talk was brilliant, but the radicals thought otherwise. They said he was a great orator, but he didn't know what he was talking about, his facts were all wrong.
> Dr. Bradley's rebuttal was so clear, so concise, so full of truth, and delivered with such charm that the radicals were discomfited. There were tears in my eyes, and a standing ovation from the audience, as he stepped down from the podium.[34]

Growing in popularity with scattered Chautauqua and lyceum audiences, speaking to congregations filling the Wilson Avenue

Theater and the Pantheon Theater, addressing civic clubs and public forums in Chicago, Preston Bradley became a prominent and powerful speaker.

But he wanted more than fame as an eloquent pulpiteer. He wanted to translate his liberal idealism into a permanent organization more cohesive than weekly theater engagements. He wanted an established institution for the purpose of ministering to a particular kind of religious personality. Dr. Bradley described the liberal whose spirit was the clergyman's principal concern as follows:

> A Liberal, when speaking in terms of its philosophical significance, is one who entertains an open mind toward all the problems involved in the experience of life. A true Liberal can never assume an attitude of impregnability toward any theory, ideal, creed, race, individual, church or system. A true Liberal can never say, "You are wrong if you do not see this matter through my eyes and comprehend it with my mind." A true Liberal never permits his intellectual variances to obscure those attractive qualities of heart and life of those who disagree with him. A true Liberal will never willingly injure his fellow-man of whatever belief. A true Liberal will never be the assassin of another's character. A true Liberal will never retaliate the "unchristian" attacks of those who are professing to be "like Christ."[35]

Dr. Bradley's autobiography contains this conviction. "In my view, the liberal is concerned with Christianity as a way, not as a creed; as a life, not as a system."[36] Recognizing the purposes which a church should serve and knowing the identity of the religious liberal to whom he especially ministered, Dr. Bradley guided his growing congregation toward the new building which he envisioned.

An historic event took place after the worship services on June 14, 1925. Following the benediction, Bradley stepped from the platform in the Pantheon Theater, assembled with the Board of Trustees, and marched in a processional which included the robed choir and the congregation. Following the unfurling of the colors of the American flag, they walked down Sheridan Road and reached Lawrence Avenue. From a struggling congregation gathered in Viking Temple and Arcola Hall, from a growing company crowding the Wilson Theater and the Pantheon Theater, the pioneering liberals finally reached a crudely erected speakers' platform within a few blocks of Lake Michigan. Dr. Bradley presented his pastoral prayer, grasped a shovel handed to him by President C. K. Anderson of the Board of Trustees, and broke the ground for the eventual erection of the People's Church of Chicago.[37]

Although Preston Bradley severed his ministerial relationship with the traditional denominations when he inaugurated an independent church, behind him were the examples of other religious nonconformists by whom he was certainly influenced.

One of America's greatest platform personalities, the agnostic Robert G. Ingersoll, exercised an important influence upon growing religious liberalism.[38] The son of a clergyman, Ingersoll moved through the Midwest as his father denounced chattel slavery. At the appointment of Governor Richard J. Oglesby, Ingersoll served as attorney general of Illinois between 1867 and 1869. He was denied nomination for governor at the Republican state convention in May, 1868. Although Ingersoll's unrepressed religious agnosticism might have contributed toward this political defeat, he secured a national reputation as a gifted speaker when he nominated James G. Blaine for the presidency at the Republican national convention in Cincinnati, Ohio, on June 15, 1876. Essentially, Ingersoll established his initial reputation as an outstanding attorney in the Midwest, secured national prominence as a political speaker, and gained enduring fame as an eloquent agnostic.

An important Chicago clergyman who encouraged Chicago's growing ecclesiastical liberalism was Robert Collyer, a popular preacher.[39] This clergyman-blacksmith emigrated to the United States from England, became a Methodist lay minister, and questioned the orthodox doctrines of man's complete depravity and the vicarious atonement. Collyer's ministerial license was withdrawn in January, 1859. In February, however, Collyer was called to Chicago as minister-at-large of the First Unitarian Church; he was ordained into the Unitarian ministry in May. The Reverend Robert Collyer became pastor of Unity Church on Chicago's north side. His pastorate flourished as Collyer developed one of Chicago's largest churches.

In October, 1871, Collyer watched a flaming inferno sweep across the Chicago River, spread through familiar neighborhoods, and destroy the magnificent ecclesiastical edifice of Unity Church.[40] This is how Collyer remembered assembling his congregation following the fire: "Then I spoke about the situation, and I told them they must pay me no stipend for the year to come. I could take care of my family, and this I would do. Could go back to the anvil at a pinch and make horseshoes, whereat they smiled and so did I."[41]

Another liberal, Professor David Swing, who was acquitted on heresy charges before withdrawing from the Chicago presbytery, resigned from the Fourth Presbyterian Church in October, 1875. Eventually fifty Chicago citizens each subscribed one thousand dollars to inaugurate an independent nonsectarian congregation in Chicago's heartland, with Swing as minister. Thus Central Church of Chicago was established in December, 1875, with five hundred members. Moving from an initial group meeting in McVickers Theater, a growing congregation convened in the Central Music Hall and became "the most famous independent church in Chicago," while Swing was acknowledged as "one of the great liberal preachers of his day."[42]

When Professor Swing conducted his controversial ministry, an independent congregation assembling in McVickers Theater under ministerial leadership from a former Methodist minister, Dr. Hiram W. Thomas, inaugurated a Peoples Church. Dr. Thomas' struggle with Methodism brought charges of heresy.

> At the 1878 session charges were preferred against Dr. H. W. Thomas, pastor of Centenary Church, Chicago, involving charges of heresy. This was the beginning of the most famous heresy trial in the history of the conference. The original charges were held in abeyance. But the agitations against Dr. Thomas continued. In 1880 a paper was presented calling on him to withdraw from the Methodist ministry and pledging the conference to "commend him to God, to the word of His grace and to the guidance of the Holy Spirit, who leads into all truth." An attempt was made and failed to substitute a motion calling for a special committee to try

him. The original question was called. Dr. Thomas addressed the conference and the original motion was presented and sustained by a vote of 110 to 65.

Dr. Thomas followed this vote to withdraw with a refusal to do so, supported by a long defense of his doctrines and a plea for the historic liberty of thought which had characterized Methodism. . . .

The committee on Thomas expelled him from the ministry and membership of the Methodist Episcopal Church.[43]

From this congregation with Dr. Thomas, according to a memorial history published by the Peoples Church, came the present world-famous institution.

The Peoples Church of Chicago was founded more than 88 years ago by Dr. Hiram Thomas who, because of his liberal theological viewpoint, found himself out of sympathy with the theology of Methodism. As the pastor of a Methodist Church in Chicago, his liberal point of view put him constantly on the defensive within the pattern of his own denominational theology. He finally withdrew from the Methodist Church and founded the Peoples Church of Chicago.[44]

That Preston Bradley regarded Hiram W. Thomas as the founder was attested to in the following way:

Dr. Bradley regards this group—founded by Dr. Hiram Thomas, another liberal churchman—as the real genesis of his church. "I didn't found Peoples Church," he says, "and I want to clear this up."[45]

IV. Public Tributes and Family Occasions

Through the years came numerous public recognitions, times for celebration and commemoration, acclamations shared as personal occasions and family observances. Public tributes honoring Preston Bradley became reciprocal compliments between a pastor and his congregation.

Beloved by known and unknown persons whose lives were inspired by his ministry, Dr. Preston Bradley's life was deeply involved with Grace Wilkins Thayer, whom he married on November 25, 1915; their foster son, James Bradley-Griffin; and his second wife, June Haslet, whom he wedded on June 30, 1952. Countless moments of relaxation and recreation with his family occured at Arden Lodge on Black Duck Island in Lake Vermillion near Tower, Minnesota.

Grace Thayer Bradley, the daughter of William Thayer, a foreign buyer with the Marshall Field Company, gave strength of purpose to Preston's early ministry. Preston and Grace were introduced by Miss Frances Norton, a daughter of editor Colonel Norton of the *Chicago Record Herald*. They were married in the Bradley's apartment on Clarendon Avenue on Thanksgiving Day, November 25, 1915. Following Mrs. Bradley's death on May 27, 1950, Dr. Bradley recalled their first meeting in the Thayer home on Aldine Square in this way:

> We entered the home that evening and as we stepped into the hall, I looked up the long stairway that led to the second floor, and there she stood. As she walked down the stairs to greet us and our friend presented us, I thought she was one of the loveliest and most refined young ladies I had ever met, and she was!
>
> It was a warm evening and I remember later on, when we were served a light repast, she said, "I learned from Frances you like buttermilk," and she brought out a pitcher of cold buttermilk. Strange how these little things come back to one, etched as they have been in memory and forgotten until memory recreates the yesterdays of life.[46]

Grace Bradley sustained her husband's ministry. She served as charter member, corresponding secretary, and honorary president for the Women's Club of the Peoples Church of Chicago. Also, she edited the church's monthly magazine, the *Liberal*, later the *Liberalist,* when it first appeared in April, 1924. After entering Ravenswood Hospital on March 16, 1950, Mrs. Bradley responded satisfactorily before relapsing with lobar pneumonia and passing away at 8:30 Saturday evening, May 27, 1950.[47]

The Reverend and Mrs. Bradley adopted a handsome, artistic, talented son, James Bradley-Griffin. When James' father, Dr. G. H.

Griffin, died, Mrs. Griffin entered the United States from England, where Jimmy was born at Bradford on June 29, 1901. He excelled in drama and music at Lake View High School, then continued his education at Northwestern University and Beloit College. James gained national recognition as the director of the Uptown Players, a dramatics company affiliated with the Peoples Church. The Uptown Players gave impetus to the present burgeoning little-theater movement in the United States. James died on Black Duck Island in Minnesota on Saturday, May 26, 1951.

The deaths of Grace Thayer Bradley and James Bradley-Griffin left Preston Bradley grief stricken but mellowed with a compassionate sensitivity through which he could sympathize more deeply with sorrowful mourners.

V. Rebirth of the Peoples Church of Chicago

When the Reverend Dr. Bradley awoke at dawn on October 10, 1926, he peered through the early morning mist which settled across enshrouded, leaden-colored Lake Michigan. Dr. Bradley was momentarily disappointed; the splendid autumnal beauty of Saturday was not extended through dedicatory Sunday, the first services in the new auditorium. He described his feelings in the September, 1926, *Liberal*.

> There are moments when I feel overwhelmed when I think of the thousands who have come under the influence of our church in all of these years. I think of their sorrow and failures, joy and victories, and often wonder how life has treated them. The thought of it all humiliates as well as inspires me. I can close my eyes now and visualize some of those great Sunday mornings together. I often think of our first Sunday service after war was declared. I can never forget that Sunday morning just before I left for Europe, and my throat tightens even now when I see through the memories of the years the congregation in the old Wilson Avenue Theater all rise as I came on the platform for the first service after my return.[48]

When the Reverend and Mrs. Preston Bradley walked down Sheridan Road and reached Lawrence Avenue on October 10, 1926, their excitement and expectations were stimulated by the pending dedication. Turning the corner, they saw the stately Romanesque playhouse auditorium; the attractive gold and white color scheme was enhanced by the dark walnut panelling. Modern theater seats arranged in abbreviated semicircles across the inclined floor seemed dramatic in contrast to the regular, evenly rowed pews in the traditional churches. The extended mezzanine and towering balcony permitted a growing congregation to view the elevated platform from the main floor. A quotation from William Ellery Channing was inscribed between two organ-pipe sets spaced above the platform which held the minister and the choir.[49] Channing's quotation stated: "Live a life of faith and hope. Believe in the mighty power of Truth and Love." The quotation was later replaced with an unusual mural which depicted the Master preaching to forty-one larger-than-life-size figures representing persons from all walks of life and every race. The mural, entitled "Keep Looking Up," is twenty-five feet high and fifteen feet wide. Painted by Louis Grell, it was donated by Leonard Hicks, vice president and managing director of Chicago's Pick-Congress Hotel. Ralph Schoenleben described the physical edifice, which, he said,

> resembles a beautiful playhouse. It has an inclined floor, theater seats instead of pews, and a very large balcony. The choir is banked at the back of a sort of stage. Dr. Bradley's "pulpit" is but a simple desk.[50]

The theatrical atmosphere characteristic of motion-picture houses like the Pantheon was extended into the permanent residence for the Peoples Church.

On that initial dedicatory Sunday, the nearly two thousand seats were filled when the congregation sang Hosmer's "Forward Through the Ages," listened briefly to Mr. C. K. Anderson, read together the specially prepared dedicatory sentences, and heard the choir sing "Unfold Ye Portals" from "Redemption" by Gounod.[51] The Reverend Preston Bradley read the thirteenth chapter of First Corinthians and preached his sermon, "Modern Life and the

Church." His dedicatory prayer reflected his idealism and his gratitude.

> Bless every workman that has had a part in this structure, the heart and brain of the man who planned it and those who have followed out those plans; and may this church stand, as it stood for the past years in this city, as an open door of Liberality and Truth; may bigotry and fanaticism never escape from the lips of its minister today or from the ministers who may serve it in the future; may it be a place in the life of this city where people feel that they can come and think for themselves in matters of religious philosophy; may it always be an open door to the downtrodden and the broken and the bruised and the bleeding and the dying and the struggling and the failing and the sorrowing and the sinning; may it be a great source of beauty and of power and of inspiration in this city for the cause of Truth and Justice.[52]

The Reverend Bradley was moved most deeply not by the surrounding congregation or the extensive radio audience; he was moved most when he saw his father sitting in the congregation and wanted to say, "We made it, Dad. We made it."[53]

The clergyman stood for an hour following the services receiving hearty congratulations from an enthusiastic congregation; but he was pleased especially with a telegram from the Reverend Carl Lundbum, pastor of Dr. Bradley's boyhood Presbyterian church in Linden, Michigan. Lundbum's congratulations symbolized the congenial cooperation and religious fraternity which prevailed unceasingly between the Chicago clergyman and the Linden Presbyterian congregation. Dr. Bradley described his Presbyterian allegiance when he preached "If" on May 21, 1961:

> I was born a Presbyterian, brought up a Presbyterian, preached my first sermon in a Presbyterian Church, and am a member of the Presbyterian Church today! My little boyhood church at Linden has never removed my name from their roll! And though I have become a religious liberal, though I have very little confidence in creeds, in dogmas and in decadent twelfth-century theology, the roots of my life and my heart are in the church of my father.[54]

The Reverend Bradley remembered his boyhood church years

later during the dedication ceremonies opening the memorial Preston Bradley Chapel; and to this Michigan congregation he returned as the invited preacher to deliver the one hundredth anniversary sermon. When he described that Sunday in his home church, he remarked:

> I found that the Presbyterian church had decided to unite with the Methodists in the service. I had been brought up in the Presbyterian Church and I was deeply touched when my old church decided to abandon its services for the day and have a union service . . . .
> We were not Presbyterians, Methodists or Unitarians in that service—we were just old friends—knowing and loving each other. That Sunday in the old home church will abide with me while life lingers.[55]

From his boyhood Presbyterian heritage, Preston Bradley drew strength; and though he withdrew from the Chicago presbytery, his dedication to spiritual values matured as he struggled to interpret and articulate a meaningful message. And the institution which grew from his ministry symbolized the principles and purpose which characterized his liberal religion. His description of the church indicated the nature of his religious convictions and commitment:

> A church without a creed, a church without a dogma, a church that doesn't compel anyone to think the way the minister thinks, or the way the church thinks, but which respects the dignity and greatness of individual thinking. A church that respects the integrity of the individual mind. A church that is undergirded with only one desire—to point men and women toward the stars, and men and women of every creed, color and race, every condition in society, the rich and the poor, the wicked and the good. The church of no distinctions, the church of the forgiving heart, the church which understands. That is the Peoples Church of Chicago.[56]

In another article, Dr. Bradley explained:

> The Peoples Church of Chicago stands solidly for the preservation of every ideal necessary to the fruition of the human personality. We believe in the sacredness and the dignity of human

life. Anything which gives value, significance and understanding to the problems of human living, we consider to be essentially religious.⁵⁷

This was the faith, the liberal religion, which Dr. Bradley proclaimed, which the Peoples Church represented, and which numerous Chicagoans found meaningful.

VI. Preaching

The powerful preaching of the unconventional clergyman soon attracted attention. William F. M'Dermott wrote in the *Chicago Daily News:* "Those with good memories say the fiery preacher from the country, who recklessly tackled the 'city problem' at the very beginning of his ministry, worked up a great sweat that made him look like a wilted sunflower by the time his sermon was over."⁵⁸ John H. Sengstacke stated in the *Chicago Defender:* "His sermons are gems of wisdom reflecting their brilliance on every crevice of human thought and action. His texts are often chosen not out of the Holy Scriptures, but out of the cold, raw facts of modern life."⁵⁹ Rabbi Lewis Mann of Sinai Temple in Chicago explained:

> He does not believe that the living dogmas of the dead should become the dead dogmas of the living! He does not promise individuals golden staircases in the hereafter and remain silent for those who never see any gold on this earth and who are continually being exploited and crushed by those above them!⁶⁰

That Dr. Bradley might have violated certain conventional rhetorical principles was indicated by this *American Magazine* comment: "By breaking most of the rules of preaching, Preston Bradley, of Chicago, has become one of the world's most successful preachers."⁶¹ Morrison explained:

> His sermon is nothing less than an event in his own soul, and

Preaching 45

when he enters his pulpit, his spirit is bowed down with the responsibility of making that sermon an event in the hearts of the troubled or indifferent or disillusioned people before him.

Preachers are not just made—they are born. And God endowed this preacher with rare gifts of personality, a mellifluous voice, imagination, a sensitive temperament, and a deep feeling for the mystery of life.[62]

VII. The Broadcasting Ministry

Dr. Bradley pioneered in radio broadcasting. The *Chicago's American* carried Earle Harvey's description of Dr. Bradley as "one of America's first radio preachers."[63] The Sunday morning worship services broadcast as an experiment in 1923 eventually became the oldest continuous church service broadcast in the United States. The preacher discussed "Some Radio Experiences" on May 16, 1937.

We are almost the last of the group of churches who started broadcasting within four or five years when we went on the air, and . . . still the opportunity for broadcasting is probably the greatest opportunity for good and at the same time the greatest responsibility in a changing order that any individual could possibly have.[64]

Bradley's effectiveness in reaching a radio listening audience is affirmed by his sustained popularity. On March 24, 1957, the *Chicago's American* indicated: "His radio broadcasts, a familiar feature of the local radio picture for the past 33 years, draw an estimated 5,000,000 listeners weekly and he receives an average of 1,000 letters a week."[65] The *Chicago Sun-Times* on October 1, 1953, noted that "for the last 30 years his voice has been a radio 'must!' "[66] These claims are sustained by these statistics reported in the *Chicago Sun* on March 14, 1945:

Chicagossip: The latest Hooper Poll, the barometer of radio, gives four firsts to Dr. Preston Bradley, pastor of the Peoples

Church, who is now in his 21st year of broadcasting—his eighth with the same sponsor. The poll gives Dr. Bradley the highest rating of any Chicago commentator on any Chicago station at any time—a 6.2 rating; the highest rating of any program on any station at 6 P.M. (when he speaks over WGN); the highest rating on any hour of any program on WJJD; the highest rating of any Chicago religious or church broadcast on any station at any hour for his Sunday 11 A.M. broadcast over WJJD.[67]

Dr. Bradley was heard nightly each week over WGN Chicago through sixteen years and over WJJD during seven continuous years. He spoke over WLS, WCFL, WEBH, WBKB, WFMF-FM, and WGN-TV during the 1960-1961 church season. Dr. Bradley alternated with Catholic Bishop Fulton J. Sheen in a weekly WGN-TV program. Effective employment of radio and television broadcasting provided an important opportunity for reaching an extensive listening audience.

His experience in radio broadcasting provides humorous happenings which enhance his unconventional ministry. Dr. Bradley was deprived of the immediate inspiration he secured from a present audience. He stated in his "Along the Way" column published in the *Liberalist* dated March 8, 1963: "How I miss an audience in making these radio recordings! There is no inspiration in sitting alone in a studio, looking through a glass window at an engineer and attempting to be inspirational."[68] He explained this sensation in his column datelined January 4, 1963.

> Sitting in a studio, looking through a glass window at an engineer and a director, and trying to be inspirational and helpful! That is a challenge which I face every time I make a recording. Audiences inspire me. People surrounding me when I am speaking lift me up. One gets a reaction and response from their faces.[69]

His datelined entry for Friday, April 17, 1964, reported a wedding he conducted in WFMF radio studios—perhaps the first wedding ceremony solemnized on a Chicago radio station.[70] A triple simultaneous presentation facilitated by electronic equipment was reported for Sunday, April 12, 1964. While speaking personally at Trinity Lutheran Church, he delivered an invocation and address via tape recordings for the WLS Old-timers' Party at the Sherman House and presented his regular vespers service over WCFL![71]

His sermons indicate that his broadcasting exerted an incredible influence upon the lives of the listening audience. Reaching persons through broadcasting destroyed certain communication barriers; sectarian exclusiveness was diminished when Protestants heard Roman Catholic priests for the first time, while Jews heard Protestant clergymen, and Protestants heard rabbis. When Dr. Bradley discussed "Some Radio Experiences" on May 16, 1937, he reported:

> Every week of my life I am preaching funeral sermons for people I have never seen, for families with whom I have never been, and I never refuse them whatever help or comfort I can give. Sometimes when I am so physically exhausted that I can hardly pull myself together I answer the call. Whether it is a humble dwelling or a palatial home makes no difference to me. And the sick people with whom I have talked for years over long periods of illness—it has been my privilege to visit them by the scores and hundreds; and I would rather have that influence on the radio than be a member of the passing show.[72]

A specific example of Dr. Bradley's popularity was evidenced when he entered a diner on a Burlington railroad train, discovered that the bill of fare commemorated the twenty-fifth anniversary of the congregation, and learned that many of the diners were friends or members of the Peoples Church of Chicago.[73]

With the development of television, Dr. Bradley made guest appearances on popular Chicago programs, and the church services were telecast occasionally. Taped highlights from the fiftieth anniversary celebration of the Peoples Church were broadcast over WGN and WGN-TV in 1962.

Preston Bradley recognized the significance of public opinion in America, and he employed a multiplicity of mass media in communicating his religious liberalism. His consciousness of the effectiveness of mass media was evident in these words:

> I have said it repeatedly and I say it again, that the greatest

power in a democracy is public opinion. The newspaper, the editor, the commentator, the educator, the minister, the priest, the rabbi, the teacher, those who have the responsibility of creating public opinion, they are the most powerful people in the world.[74]

He amplified this assumption when he said that "the greatest power in a democracy is the institution or the individual who has the responsibility of creating public opinion."[75] While towering, needlelike antennae from cosmopolitan skyscrapers projected blazing neon insignia from a seashore horizon, the influences from broadcasting prompted Bradley to criticize the power of these communication instruments upon human individuality and originality.

> I think the greatest need of this world today and the greatest need of this American nation at this moment is people of pioneering mind. The trouble is we are becoming stamped with mass communications—mass communications in television . . . in radio . . . in books . . . in the air. We are reading the same things, responding and reacting in the same way, until the courage of individual, original speaking is almost dead.[76]

Dr. Bradley was concerned that mass-media communication be employed to promote individual freedom of thought and expression and the democratic process in human society. He became apprehensive that broadcasting might become an influence suppressing human personality and human values in a technological culture and mechanical environment.

VIII. *Author and Critic*

While employing radio and television broadcasting to communicate his messages, Dr. Bradley published ten books. Bobbs-Merrill published *Courage for Today* in 1934, *Mastering Fear* in 1935, and *Power From Right Thinking* in 1936. Harper's edition of *Life and You* followed in 1937. The Peoples Church published Dr. Bradley's edition of collected prayers, entitled *Meditations,* in 1941. In the same year Stokes added *New Wealth for You.* Wilcox and Follett presented Dr. Bradley's *My Daily Strength* in 1943. Permabook's paperback *Meditations and My Daily Strength* was published in 1946, and an edition of *Meditations* was published in 1946 by Wilcox and Follett. Dr. Bradley's sermon "Life's Deeper Meanings" was included in George Paul Butler's *Best Sermons* in 1946 by Harpers. Hanover House published *Happiness Through Creative Living* in 1955. David McKay published Dr. Bradley's autobiographical *Along the Way,* on which he collaborated with Harry Barnard, on September 21, 1962; this day was celebrated in Chicago and throughout Illinois as the fiftieth anniversary of the Reverend Bradley's ministry. On May 3, 1967, Aspley House honored Dr. Bradley's fifty-fifth anniversary in the ministry by publishing his *Between You and Me.* The Chicago chapter of the Friends of Literature honored Dr. Bradley during the eleventh annual Shakespeare Birthday Program and Awards Dinner at Chicago's Blackstone Hotel on May 9, 1942; their citation praised the clergyman for his service to literature

> as exemplified by the excellence of his contributions to the literary life of the age through the nobility of his own writings; his sympathetic evaluation of the writings of his predecessors and contemporaries; and his inspirational lectures which have encouraged thousands to read good books.[77]

For thirty-eight consecutive years Dr. Bradley presided as master of ceremonies at this Shakespeare Birthday Program and Awards Dinner.

Perhaps Dr. Bradley's most important contribution to Chicago's literary life was the Wednesday evening book reviews he presented at the Peoples Church. The *Daily News* on June 8, 1940, reported that the Wednesday evening book talks were the best-attended reviews in America,[78] and this series eventually became the oldest series of book lectures in Chicago. Dorothy Dockstader described Bradley's book reviews this way in the *Publishers' Weekly:*

It is not unusual for the church auditorium holding 1,700 people to be completely filled by seven thirty or earlier for an eight o'clock lecture. People begin to arrive at six o'clock. The lectures are not broadcast.

The total attendance for the series of 34 lectures, according to actual statistics kept by the church, was 38,390 . . . an average of 1,555 per lecture. This includes no count of the hundreds who were turned away for lack of space in the church.[79]

From a questionnaire distributed to half the audience attending the last book review of the series, Dorothy Dockstader discovered that seventy percent of the people who attended the lectures read between one and twenty-three of the books Dr. Bradley reviewed; that thirty percent read none; and that thirty-one percent purchased books. Two thousand one hundred persons heard Bradley's reviews of *The Mother* and *On Our Way,* the largest audiences during the series. As an individual, Dr. Preston Bradley exercised a remarkable influence upon the reading of books; he carried books around with him and enjoyed discussing them before audiences which swelled to two thousand.

IX. *Highlights Along the Way*

The twenty-fifth anniversary of the Peoples Church of Chicago was commemorated with a silver jubilee banquet at Chicago's Palmer House on April 15, 1937.[80] The mounting excitement and growing expectancy commenced when arriving crowds packed the spacious hallway leading to the Grand Ballroom thirty minutes before the doorways were opened. Promptly at seven o'clock Dr. and Mrs. Bradley and the members of the Board of Trustees, with their wives, entered, accompanying the distinguished guests. An immediate standing ovation erupted in reverberating applause. A shimmering silvery drapery suspended from the ceiling formed a backdrop, while silver letters illumined electrically announced, "Twenty-fifth Anniversary." The dinner culminated with a dramatic climax when frozen dessert was served on ice blocks which concealed colored lights; hundreds of frozen cakes, carried in an awe-inspiring procession, were introduced by three white-garbed chefs who carried huge frozen designs above their heads. The lighting was dimmed into darkness. Eventually, following a tumultuous storm of thundering applause, Dr. Bradley stood, gazed across the engulfing expanse of human faces, and struggled for words to communicate a grateful response.

Several honorary doctorates acclaimed the clergyman's career. Grace Thayer Bradley and James Bradley-Griffin watched when Preston Bradley was presented an honorary doctrate of laws from Lake Forest College on June 11, 1938.[81] On Monday evening, June 12, 1939, similar honors were awarded during academic ceremonies at an associated theological seminary of the federated faculties at the University of Chicago.[82] Dr. Preston Bradley delivered a baccalaureate address and received an honorary divinity doctorate from Yankton College on June 5, 1966. He received the L.H.D. degree from Lincoln Memorial University on June 9, 1968, and the Litt.D. from Lincoln College on February 7, 1971.

The Reverend Dr. Bradley was adopted into a Chippewa Indian tribe during two-day ceremonies held on an Indian reservation near Lake Vermillion on an especially hot Sunday, July 21, 1940.[83] When Dr. Bradley presented the tribe with a blanket and smoking tobacco expressing his good will, Chief Good-Day bestowed upon the clergyman the Indian name "Misi-we-gwa-neb," which means "a feather from every kind of bird all over the world." Dr. Bradley was given a gorgeous chieftain's headdress composed of forty brown eagle feathers, fluffy white maribou feathers, a red and white beaded forehead band, and red leather strands hanging across his shoulders.

X. Dimensions of Ministry

Besides his dramatic preaching, Dr. Bradley's physical appearance and popular appeal attracted public attention. Ralph Schoenleben wrote:

> A short, rotund, swarthy man walked rapidly into the lobby of a hotel. His thick crop of hair was much too long. His appearance was commanding....
>
> His fearless attacks on isolationist extremists, and his ceaseless campaigns against defeatism, are in no small degree responsible for the balance of the otherwise isolationistic Midwest.
>
> He is far and away America's most popular lecturer....
>
> Who is this dynamic little man who has held his popularity for thirty years in a town in which the average pastorate is but seven years, who in his early fifties is regarded by some as the greatest living American?[84]

Schoenleben further stated:

> He will bury, gratis, the reprobates no other minister would touch. He knows, and is loved by people in every department of life. The newsboy who hands him the paper on his way to church says, "I don't want no money for it." The Pullman porters take up a collection among themselves so his meal on the diner may be free. A western tribe of Indians has made him an honorary chief.[85]

Newspaperman Herb Graffis reported: "Many times he has been the Front Man for the backsliders at the last sad rites and [has] given the widow of a late almost unlamented the ten bucks that an opulent survivor passed to Preston for the services."[86]

Earl Nightingale wrote:

> Every minute of his days and a goodly share of his nights, seven days a week, this happy man of God can be found working in his Middle-Western garden of human beings. Preaching in his crowded church; counselling the numberless who have found the burden of today's living too great to bear alone; speaking to jammed auditoriums, television cameras and radio microphones; or standing with a knot of mourners in a cemetery under a snow-threatening sky—Dr. Bradley is, to my mind, one of our most remarkable Americans.[87]

On April 8, 1957, *Newsweek* said:

> Dr. Bradley cuts a startling figure. Widely known for his varied collections of walking-sticks and pipes—mostly gifts—he is

5-foot-5½, chunky, and sports a frock coat, black trousers, and a loose, black bow tie. Aged 68, he brushes his hair back in an electric gray-white shock.[88]

A small northern Minnesota newspaper, the *Mesabi Daily News*, reported:

In his hey-day Dr. Bradley cut a striking figure with his black suit, white shirt and black tie when he appeared on numerous platforms throughout the area, selling the Arrowhead to local residents and protecting it from those who would spoil its wilderness aspects.[89]

On October 15, 1967, Connie Meyers described Dr. Bradley thus: "A twinkly man with a round cherubic face and a halo of white hair, he always wears a small bow tie."[90]

But Dr. Bradley's physical appearance and actions consisted neither of theatrical showmanship contrived as ministerial entertainment nor the ecclesiastical dramatics of a frustrated actor. Rather the minister's unconventional but characteristic demeanor was an authentic expression revealing the spontaneous individuality and irrepressible originality of the religious rebel whom Carl I. Henrikson described this way:

In pioneering through uncharted fields of thought, the seeker after the good, the true and the beautiful frequently finds himself "at odds" with things, as though the world were out of joint and there were no answers to his cries in the wilderness. In this mood of frustration he recognizes a choice between surrender before the tidal wave of standardization and a "going it alone" with brave assertions of individuality. He suddenly realizes that he is a rebel—not in a political but in a psychological sense—a rebel against prevailing injustices, the euphemisms of hypocrisy, and the deadening platitudes of mediocrity.[91]

Creativity in reformulating theological conceptions was consistent with the creativity that Dr. Bradley manifested in his physical appearance.

Dr. Bradley's personal habits and professional routine were noticed by newspaper and magazine reporters. *Time* stated on

April 26, 1937: "Preston Bradley, 48, drinks lemon juice before breakfast, walks an hour a day, spends his vacations piloting his 30-ft. cruiser on the lakes of northern Minnesota."[92]

Schoenleben described Dr. Bradley's morning routine with these words:

> Preston Bradley rises at six o'clock in the morning. After a few minutes of meditation to fortify himself for the day, he flicks on his bedside radio to get the latest news while dressing. He wears the same style and color suit year in year out. His little black bow ties, he buys by the dozen.
> Breakfast is preceded by a glass of lemon juice. Then Preston Bradley begins the daily round of conferences, lectures, broadcasts, marriages, funerals, sick calls, which earn him the title of "Busiest man in the country."[93]

On April 8, 1957, *Newsweek* mentioned Dr. Bradley's extensive, demanding duties, saying:

> Dr. Bradley finds time for a wide range of parish duties. He conducts about five weddings and as many funerals a week, speaks four or five times to public gatherings, and calls on all sick members of his congregation of 3,850. He also gives a Wednesday night book lecture in the church, edits his church monthly, the *Liberalist*, and still saves an hour a day for a walk.
> To maintain this pace, Dr. Bradley is chauffeured about in a Cadillac given him two years ago by a friend. In a state where drivers place a high value on low license-plate numbers, Dr. Bradley does pretty well with his No. 9.[94]

Another *Newsweek* quotation, dated October 1, 1962, illustrates his steady pace thus:

> Even for Dr. Preston Bradley, the pace last week was fast. At the age of 74, the pint-size pastor of the Peoples Church of Chicago found time and energy to tape his biweekly television show and some of his fifteen weekly radio broadcasts, consult with the publishers of his ninth and newest book (an autobiography), write an editorial and a sermon for his monthly magazine, explain why he declined to be a candidate for Congress this fall, speak at half a dozen luncheons and dinners, attend civic committee meetings, conduct weddings and funerals, and visit all those in his 4,000-member congregation who were ill.[95]

Dimensions of Ministry 55

Exhaustive daytime and evening engagements, schedules arranged sometimes a year in advance, consumed the clergyman's energies and efforts.

The statistical results of Dr. Bradley's ministry indicate its dimension. The *Chicago Daily News,* on June 8, 1940, said: "A metropolitan church that has grown from a handful of people to a membership of 3,431, with an additional radio roll of 8,000, making a total of more than 11,300 listed adherents, will honor its pastor-founder for his 28 years of leadership tomorrow."[96]

M'Dermott described Dr. Bradley's congregation in the *Chicago Daily News* on March 21, 1942, in this way:

> On Sunday morning the visitor would see a full church; at night 2,000 packed into the auditorium and hall below, which is served by an amplifying system, and 1,000 turned away for lack of room—this in the face of the fact that most churches have closed down their evening devotions.[97]

American Magazine, in April, 1943, announced: "He follows no ritual, conducts no membership drives, never mentions sectarian doctrine. But he packs 2,200 persons into his church each Sunday, has a radio audience estimated at 5,000,000, and receives 1,000 letters a week."[98] The *Chicago Sunday Times* stated on April 20, 1947: "In his 35 years as a pastor, the popular preacher has conducted more than 2,500 funerals and performed more than 2,000 marriage ceremonies. He has christened at least 1,000 children."[99] On June 8, 1946, the *Chicago Daily News* reported: "His 60 to 70 commitments a month bring him a six-figure salary so that he is the highest-paid clergyman anywhere on the air today."[100] The *Chicago Sun-Times,* on April 28, 1962, published an estimate stating that he delivers "an average of 200 speeches a year," and that he had conducted forty-five summer preaching tours through Europe.[101]

Dr. Bradley's extensive engagements stimulated Chicago newspaper columnist Herb Graffis to call him "the most active man in the city's public service."[102] *Newsweek,* on October 1, 1962, commended Dr. Bradley, recognizing that "for 50 years, he has been the city's leading voice of liberal Protestantism."[103] Writing in the *Chicago Daily News* on August 16, 1958, Dave Mead called Dr. Bradley "the dean of Chicago's liberal clergy."[104] Stanley Pieza speculated in the *Chicago's American* on April 28, 1962: "His 50 years in the same pulpit is a record of continuous pastoral service perhaps unmatched in Chicago by a congregation leader of any faith."[105]

XI. Involvement in the Life of His Time

The pulpit of the Peoples Church was a place from which the Reverend Dr. Bradley articulated his beliefs on controversial public questions. And the clergyman actually became involved in social movements, which he described in *Along the Way*.

> In 1919, I marched with Jane Addams and others for the right of women to vote. I spoke out against the Ku Klux Klan in the 1920's so vigorously that for weeks the Chicago police assigned bodyguards to me because they feared I would be attacked. In the 1930's I defended—most of the time—the economic reforms of the Roosevelt New Deal. I spoke out against Hitler. I am proud that Herr Hitler in 1937 refused to let me visit Germany. In 1945 I participated in international politics as a citizen delegate to the San Francisco conference for establishing the United Nations Organization.[106]

During the summer the Scopes Trial pitted William Jennings Bryan against Clarence Darrow, the *Herald and Examiner* stated on May 23, 1925: "Dr. Preston Bradley, pastor of the Peoples Church of Chicago, discussing the controversy over evolution in Tennessee, declared the controversy is an indictment of the most sacred of American institutions—the right to think."[107] On March 5, 1945, the *Chicago Sun* reported Dr. Bradley's opposition to the proposed peacetime military conscription.[108] The *Chicago Daily Tribune,* on November 10, 1941, stated that Dr. Bradley "branded as appropriate to Nazism or communism" the announcement of Colonel Early E. W. Duncan of Denver, Colorado; Duncan had threatened to declare off bounds any churches where sermons opposing President Roosevelt were delivered.[109] When G. L. K. Smith attempted to secure a hall in which to speak, the *Chicago Sun,* on March 13, 1945, reported that Dr. Bradley released a statement signed by thirty thousand persons who protested against the introduction of Nazi-like forces of intolerance.[110] On June 15, 1953, the *Chicago's American* reported that Preston Bradley joined an appeal to President Eisenhower requesting clemency for condemned atomic spies Julius and Ethel Rosenberg.[111] The *Chicago's American,* on April 24, 1957, noted that Dr. Bradley and Superior Judge Sbarbaro recommended Nathan Leopold's release from Stateville Prison.[112] On January 18, 1965, the *Chicago Sun-Times* announced that Dr. Bradley supported the removal of the statute of limitations which prohibited further prosecution of undetected Nazis.[113] He stated his position in specific controversial cases.

The Reverend Dr. Bradley grew in political stature and public popularity. He declined a bid from Republicans in 1935 and from Democrats in 1939 to seek the mayorship of Chicago.[114] *Current Biography 1956* stated:

> During 1936 Dr. Bradley, who frequently travels abroad, was refused admission to Germany by Chancellor Adolph Hitler. In the same year, some 10,000 Chicagoans signed a petition urging the clergyman to seek nomination for mayor of Chicago on the Republican ticket, a request he did not accept.[115]

The *Chicago Sun-Times,* on October 18, 1953, carried this report:

> It came out on our TV show the other night: A group of prominent Republicans has asked Dr. Preston Bradley of Peoples Church to consider becoming a candidate for mayor in 1955. The minister indicated he'd be interested only in a non-partisan (fusion) ticket.[116]

Nominations for the mayorship from Democrats and Republicans were succeeded by invitations that he seek the office of Congressman-at-Large from the state of Illinois and Congressman from the Ninth District. On September 28, 1962, he stood before the United States House of Representatives and delivered a prayer as Honorary Chaplain. According to the *Congressional Record,* the Reverend Dr. Bradley prayed:

> Infinite and Eternal Father, we are grateful that in a world bewitched by hatred, tortured by religious and racial animosities, there is this deliberative assembly trying to give proper evaluation and perspective to the great problems of our time.
> We ask Thy blessing upon it and upon every Member of this House. May we ever be sensitive to the responsibilities which are upon us in this fragile hour in the history of the world.
> We are grateful most of all for the opportunity which is presented to us in this greatest and most important parliamentary body in the world. We must stand for that which is honorable and right and just. May we respect each other's loyalties and find a great common denominator upon which we can build and find our way back again to dignity, to greatness, and to peace.
> In the spirit of love we pray, and for love's dear sake. Amen.[117]

When the revered clergyman returned to the pulpit the following Sunday morning, he reflected upon the event this way:

> On Friday of this past week I spent the whole day as the Chaplain of the National House of Representatives in Washington. I stood at the desk where the Presidents of the United States stand when they give their messages to the Congress. I stood where kings and potentates and Prime Ministers have stood—where Roosevelt and Churchill stood.[118]

The man who thus stood where Roosevelt and Churchill stood was an appropriate nominee as a citizen-advisor to the United States delegation which convened in the San Francisco Charter Convention of the United Nations. The man who was appointed by the Secretary of State of the United States remembered the experience when he preached "Red or Dead" on October 22, 1961.

> Sixteen years ago on this very night I was on a train bound for the Pacific Coast. Accompanying me were some of the members of

Involvement in the Life of His Time

the United States delegation which had been appointed for the United Nations Charter Convention: Mr. Harold Stassen, who at the time was very much in the public eye; Senator Vandenberg of the State of Michigan; and many other representatives of this nation. It was a special train. The Secretary of State had appointed me an advisor to the State Department for the Convention.[119]

When he reflected upon this experience in 1957, however, he seemed dissatisfied with a man-made institution designed to secure world peace.

I have seen all the organizations of men fail. I went through the first League of Nations. I attended the conference of the United Nations and saw men sitting at long green-covered tables trying to settle the problems of the world. I am still seeing men anchored to the philosophy that it can be done with organizations and committees and groups.[120]

Instead he proposed the following alternative:

There is a way. It will have to be the Way of Christ. I am not interested in creeds, labels, intellectual distinctions and the niceties of philosophers; I am not interested in all that. Human hearts and human lives are breaking and the world is being drenched in tears because of oil—because of men wanting to be free. We must find a way to human hearts. We must put a vacant chair at all the conference tables, wherever they may be, and when the people gather to be seated and they say: "Why, who is going to sit here? What candidate? What foreign minister? What diplomat?" Then let the people stop quarreling, and let all the churches say: "Make way for the King! The King of men's souls! Make way for the one who said: 'I am the way, I am the truth, I am the light!'" I have come to the conclusion there is no other way.[121]

From the floor of the United States Congress to the conference tables of the United Nations, Preston Bradley extended the ministry of good-will among men.

The dean of Chicago's clergymen never ignored the importance of committee action as an avenue for promoting human welfare; indeed, few men labored harder in more community committees to secure the realization of a better human society.

For forty-five years he served as a board member of the Chicago public library; for more than twenty-five years he was a member of the State Teachers College Board. Dr. Bradley was a charter member of the Chicago Commission on Human Relations, and he served with Bishop Shiel as co-chairman of the Chicago Council against Racial and Religious Discrimination. He was appointed by the governor as a member of the Prison Investigation Commission of Illinois. He served three consecutive terms as national president of the Izaak Walton League of America; he was a founder-member who gave the organization its name. He holds memberships in the Adventurer's Club, the Chicago Historical Society, and the Chicago Art Institute.

From his extensive and intense participation in community improvement and religious ministry, the Reverend Dr. Bradley accumulated numerous memorials. A recently refurnished upstairs room in Jane Addams' Hull House on the University of Illinois Chicago Circle campus, preparations to establish a Shiawassee River memorial park financed by the Preston Bradley Memorial Fund, and an annual award in speech presented at Alma College honor Dr. Bradley's achievements. There were even unconventional expressions of appreciation to indicate his strong influence. The proprietor of the Rainbow Seafood Tavern concocted a salad dressing dedicated to the minister; a grateful tobacco company created a distinctive mixture named after the clergyman and sold it for eight dollars a pound; flashing scarlet neon signs prominently displayed throughout Chicago by a commercial rug cleaning business enticed the public to listen to their radio-sponsored clergyman. His service won him the citation from the Board of Trustees of Yankton College, which presented him with an honorary divinity doctorate on June 5, 1966, summarizing his service.

> As a man of soaring spirit, you have carried the gospel message of truth and love into the hearts of millions. Your prolific mind has been the vessel into which God has whispered His will for men and from which you have interpreted and enlarged to the supreme edification of all who have heard your voice.
> As a purveyor of pulpit prowess, you have kept vital an art

that wanes in less capable hands. You are a preacher of power in an age when others would push preaching to the background of Christian witness.

As a disseminator of the written word, your books have inspired whole populations to meet their daily tasks with courage and faith.

As a founder of churches, you have gathered your flock and ministered to their needs through a half century of devotion to your ordination vows.

As a man of the universal spirit, we may call the planet Earth your home and [say] that you are God's Humanitarian-in-Residence, having elevated a common concern of brotherly love to cosmic proportions.[122]

For more than half a century, the persuasive clergyman labored as minister, serving his congregation, standing independent from ecclesiastical associations which would restrict his autonomous, congregational church.

The Reverend Bradley's ministry nurtured the liberal nonsectarian institution which developed around his preaching and personality. Few institutions in the United States exceed the Peoples Church of Chicago as the lengthened shadow from one man. Ministering to human beings congested beneath towering neon-lighted skyscrapers and within tenement-ridden poverty-stricken ghettos, he served as "the people's pastor." His sensitivity toward human need and human nature prompted him to define religion neither as a creed, a church, an association, nor an altar, but as something spiritual within the hearts of men and women.

XII. Near the End of a Career

These nonsectarian commitments distinguished a liberal independent church which eventually called itself "the largest Protestant church in Chicago."[123] Nevertheless, the church remained ecclesiastically independent; as Walter F. Morse stated in the *Chicago Sun-Times* on September 23, 1962, the Peoples Church of Chicago is "an entity by itself, responsible to neither prelate nor association."[124] The *Chicago's American* presented the following summation:

> Theologically, the Rev. Dr. Bradley defies easy classification. Though his church is Unitarian in affiliation, he recently took out a personal membership in a Chicago Congregational church. He also has a membership in a Presbyterian church in Linden, Michigan, the town in which he was born on Aug. 18, 1888.
> He sees no inconsistency in this. He says:
> "I have never been and am not now a sectarian. Though ostensibly a Unitarian I've always been a theist, not a humanist. I felt that there was not enough warmth and spiritual emphasis in the western conference of Unitarianism, and so I affiliated with the Congregationalists.
> "Unitarianism," he explained, "has no doctrinal imperatives. Some members don't believe in God at all." He added:
> "But I have never been sympathetic to a negative attitude. I like to read scripture, have prayers, and sing hymns. Some of our Unitarian churches don't have a prayer. Consequently, I found myself rather lonely."[125]

In January, 1956, Dr. Bradley gained membership in the First Congregational Church in Ravenswood, at 1722 West Montrose, where the Reverend Dr. Morrison J. Thomas served Dr. Bradley as "my pastor." Dr. Bradley's disgust with ultra-liberal Unitarians who abandon belief in God and substitute meditation for prayer seemed evident.[126] He published a personal declaration of religious freedom and unity in the Chicago press, which drew congratulations from former Illinois governor and personal friend Adlai E. Stevenson. This personal letter, dated January 18, 1956, said:

> I don't know whether you heard my cheer. In case you didn't, I'm sending this note with my applause, my thanks to *you,* and my thanks to God for *you.* And it isn't the first time, either, for I say with Paul that "I thank God for every remembrance of you."[127]

The letter from Governor Stevenson was a compliment to an unconventional clergyman who persistently stood alone . . . alone, but with his message.

Near the End of a Career

On March 17, 1964, a small white chapel on the third floor of the Peoples Church was dedicated, an intimate place for quiet meditation and spiritual sanctuary.[128] When the chapel was formally dedicated, Ethel Wells Smally, who served Dr. Bradley for nearly thirty years as his study secretary, described the event this way:

> The white chapel, with its red carpeting, the pews and all the furniture of white with mahogany trim, the soft golden lighting, the red velvet dossal back of the altar, the brasses of simple elegance on the altar, the brass vase filled with white chrysanthemums and gladioli . . . made a picture of restful, quiet loveliness.[129]

Dr. Bradley's remembrance during these dedication services was reflected this way:

> I thought of another little church, not much bigger than this chapel, where some of you were when I was invited to preach the hundredth anniversary service in that little village church, and I stood in the pulpit where I preached my first sermon—a church of which I am still a member and with which my family have been identified all their lives—a church of which this chapel is almost a duplicate. And so the color of this carpet, our white pews, the mahogany trim, the beautiful chancel, all of it creates memories and an atmosphere, and I think it should be dedicated to sincerity and seriousness.[130]

The church anniversaries became civic celebrations. Although his fiftieth anniversay in the pulpit was celebrated during services in the Peoples Church on April 29, 1962, a civic banquet honoring his fiftieth anniversary was given at McCormick Place on September 21, 1962.[131] Governor Otto Kerner and Mayor Richard J. Daley attended, spoke, and declared the date "Preston Bradley Day" throughout the state of Illinois and the city of Chicago. Governor Kerner called the clergyman "a great spiritual leader who has built a church and a tremendous following on the simple principles of an open mind and a forgiving heart."[132] One year before, Dr. Bradley had summarized:

> When I was first ordained a minister, I believed that man was created by God for a great purpose, that he was given the desire

and faculties to achieve that purpose, and that one day he will surely achieve it, becoming great by overcoming obstacles he may have himself produced. As time goes on, I am increasingly convinced this is true.[133]

The Reverend Dr. Preston Bradley celebrated his fifty-fifth anniversary with a civic banquet in the Pick-Congress Hotel on October 20, 1967. Honorary chairmen included Governor Kerner, Mayor Daley, Senator Everett McKinley Dirksen, Senator Charles H. Percy, millionaire W. Clement Stone, and physician Dr. Karl A. Meyer.[134] Dr. Bradley was commended by Dirksen as an individual who is certain to go down in history as one of the "greatest clergymen of all time."[135]

Summaries praising Preston Bradley's ministry came through proclamations celebrating the Chicago clergyman's fifty-fifth anniversary as the pastor of the Peoples Church. Suggestions indicating his influence upon Chicago and the world are reflected in this proclamation by Governor Otto Kerner:

> Whereas, For the past fifty-five years, Dr. Preston Bradley has delivered a forceful sermon at the Peoples Church of Chicago, and thereby changed many lives for the better, and
> Whereas, Dr. Bradley has worked regularly in a busy pastorate and has been in touch with all segments of humanity—the young and the elderly, the poor and the fortunate, and knows their problems, and
> Whereas, In his own words, "It is essential that every individual feel his own responsibility. Let us never underestimate the importance of the individual." As an individual, Dr. Preston Bradley offers thoughts for creative living which are acceptable to the religious or idealistic person in these troubled times, and
> Whereas, On the evening of Friday, October 20, 1967, the Civic Celebration Dinner will commemorate Dr. Bradley's fifty-five years in the pulpit of the Peoples Church of Chicago.
> Now, therefore, I Otto Kerner, Governor of the State of Illinois, do hereby proclaim that Friday, October 20, 1967, shall be DR. PRESTON BRADLEY AWARD 55 DAY throughout Illinois in grateful appreciation of the good works of this fine man.[136]

Governor Kerner's proclamation, and another from Mayor Richard J. Daley declaring "Dr. Preston Bradley day in Chicago," were landmark commendations. Daley's proclamation stated, in part:

> Whereas, Dr. Preston Bradley's reputation as a spiritual leader, champion of worthy causes, civic worker, author and commentator is nation-wide and gives him rank among Chicago's most distinguished citizens; and
>
> Whereas, Dr. Bradley has served, and continues to serve, his city and his country with unfailing zeal in administrative and advisory capacities having to do with education, youth welfare, social justice, cultural advancement and the general improvement of the quality of American life; and
>
> Whereas, Dr. Bradley's great erudition, warm humanity and spiritual dedication have made him a revered and much-beloved figure on the Chicago scene. . . .[137]

Dr. Bradley's accomplishments, accumulated through fifty-five years, were abundant.

Perhaps Preston Bradley's greatest happiness came from ministering among people whom he served as pastor. He managed to sustain personal relationships with his growing congregation, recognizing that "there is no relationship, probably, in this world more sacred than the relationship between a pastor and his people."[138] He wrote in *Life and You:*

> For years I have lived in the great city of Chicago. I have traveled about this nation and the world; I have read the books written by the best minds of my generation and the generations before us; I have known the leaders, great and small, of my community and the nation; but above all it has been my privilege to know the newsboy on the corner and the business man on the street, the milkman, the farmer, the man who carries the bricks to build the skyscrapers which reach into the sky, and the man who dug the ditches for the sewers beneath the streets; I have breathed the air of a free democracy and I pray it will ever be so.[139]

Dr. Bradley recognized that his ministry touched the lives of numerous persons, that an institution was inspired by his professional commitment, and that the living traditions inaugurated by his career should be preserved and perpetuated. When Dr. Bradley analyzed his forty-five years of ministry, he said:

Now, as life deepens for me, I am very conscious of the fact that I am facing the sunset, and I wish I were twenty again; I wish I had 50 years of it left; that I might be beginning all over again. I wish more than anything that I could accumulate the experience of these years and put it into the heart and mind of a young preacher of about 23 years of age, who will have 45 or 50 years ahead of him.[140]

On September 15, 1963, he remarked during "In Deep Waters": "In the old religious places, as they ran across Greece to the Temple of Olympus they handed the torch to the next runner. That's all I can do now, is just hand the torch to the next runner."[141]

XIII. Toward a Common Humanity

Thus the Reverend Dr. Bradley's personality became inextricably, inseparably associated with the lives of countless Chicagoans for whom "he is as much a part of the great city as Lake Michigan."[142] The *Chicago's American* stated:

> The Chicago area boasts many natural wonders, such as parks, beaches, lakeshore, rivers, and lagoons. But none is shared and enjoyed by more people daily, weekly, or yearly than the one named the Rev. Dr. Preston Bradley.[143]

Charles Clayton Morrison summarized:

> Preston Bradley belongs to Chicago. Not merely because he lives here, but because he has identified himself with so many of the nobler aspects of our civic life. He is a veritable incarnation of the spirit of Chicago—that spirit which is engaged in building a culture upon the solid foundation of our economic and industrial greatness.[144]

Bradley was Chicago in miniature, the epitome of the city, a representative of Chicago's seething spirit.

Dr. Bradley's influence, however, was not confined to Chicago; he transcended confined geographical identification by embracing an enlarged international fraternity. During the summers he traveled regularly through Europe, visiting, during 1967, Iceland, Norway, Sweden, Denmark, Finland, Germany, Scotland, Ireland, and England. A twentieth-century Socratic world citizen, he affirmed a common humanity.

> I have passed with reverence, often, through Westminster Abbey. I have stood at the graves of Victor Hugo and Voltaire. I have stood in the presence of the remaining resting home of Darwin and Browning, and all the others. I have visited in the "Church of the Presidents" and stood between the bodies of the two Adamses. I have visited the Unknown Soldiers' graves in nine countries of the world.[145]

Returning to Chicago following the first of two three-month around-the-world tours which he took during the winters of 1965 and 1966, he reconstructed some of his ventures.

> When I stood a little while ago with Mrs. Bradley on a little ship in the Ganges River, just a few feet from shore, I saw those pilgrims, wrapped in their white robes, come down the steps to bathe in the Ganges River. . . . When I walked with beggars in Benares, I saw with my own eyes the stirring of revolt. . . . We stood just a few days ago at the rail of a great ship in Hong Kong Harbor, and I saw a little mother in a sampan, working one oar of the ship with one arm, and the other holding a great long pole with a net on the end of it up to the ship to get our pennies and nickles that might be thrown into it. I saw the face of that mother and I saw the face of the baby strapped to her back, and I wondered about the future of Hong Kong.[146]

He traveled a war-weary world, sensitive and compassionate toward human suffering, learning that in the universal language of the human spirit, a baby's cry sounds the same in any language.

Committed to the integrity of individual intellectual freedom, which never substitutes bland conformity to conventional creeds for the sovereignty of personal thought, he stood alone and spoke a message. He sought an enduring immortality through an engagement of ministry toward human spirits. As he said when he delivered "If I Had Only One Sermon to Preach" on January 23, 1966:

> I want it to be said of me after I am gone and the last sermon has been preached and the last experience of life has been lived— I would rather have written upon any remnant that I leave this sentence, than any other: "He tried to be a friend of all mankind." I would rather have that said of me, than to have written the best book of my generation, than to have preached the greatest sermon; I would rather have it said of me than to command great wealth or great power, "He was a friend of man."[147]

The universal nonsectarian religious liberalism which the Reverend Dr. Bradley preached drew a growing congregation to the Peoples Church of Chicago. Perhaps he attracted more friends among the Jewish people, the Roman Catholics, and all branches of Protestant Christianity than any other pastor in a Chicago pulpit. The *Chicago's American* reported: "He lectures in synagogues and Buddhist temples and is a great admirer of Billy Graham, the evangelist, the late Pope John, and others of diverse theological viewpoints."[148] On April 4, 1964, the *Chicago Sun-Times* reported that Dr. Bradley was scheduled to speak at a Wesak festival celebrating the birthday of Gautama Buddha at the Buddhist Temple in Chicago and that Dr. Bradley had befriended the Buddhists eighteen years earlier when they were struggling to establish themselves.[149] Bradley described his relationship with the Buddhists in these words:

> Today was Buddha's birthday. He was born 2,508 years ago on April 8, in the beautiful Garden of Lumbini, located north of Benares in northeast India. The birthday is observed in what is called the Wesak Festival, which means the "Month of Flower" or "Dawn of Spring." The Buddhist Temple of Chicago, which is only a few blocks from our own church, observes this Wesak Festival with a very pretentious program. This evening was their 18th observance of it and for the past several years they have invited me to give the address. It is always a great experience.[150]

On January 13, 1963, Dr. Bradley preached "The Pope—Man of the Year." This was a significant moment in American Protestantism—when a Protestant minister eulogized a pope during a regular Sunday morning worship service. Dr. Bradley proclaimed: "In religion the things that unite people are vastly more important than the things which divide them."[151]

XIV. Arden

During Dr. Bradley's ministry, he found sanctuary and seclusion in his island home on Black Duck Island in Lake Vermillion, near Tower, Minnesota. The enchanted Forest of Arden in Shakespearean literature prompted a name for this primeval Chippewa haunt, situated six hundred miles north of Chicago. Grace Thayer Bradley described the setting this way:

> The ground is soft and "cushiony" with layer upon layer of bark and needles of pine, balsam and cedar which have dropped for no one knows how many years; there is no sound of treading feet as one walks, it is as hushed as thick velvet carpet; and when wet after a rain or in bright afternoon sunshine the ground is the richest copper color, and smells as sweet as a jar of incense.[152]

Ethel Wells Smalley recorded her impressions in these words:

> As we turned down the mossy "B" lane last summer, and the silent, piney woods closed in upon us, I felt that this Cathedral aisle must lead to the very heart of the Forest of Arden. All city life shut out and far away, I entered a new sweet world. The lane ended in a cloistered, ferny room, where a white deer lick gleamed before us like a snowy alabaster altar in the woods.
> As I stepped through a narrow hall-way of birches, out onto the mainland dock, Lake Vermillion shimmered in the sunlight, with Black Duck Island rising out of it less than a mile away.[153]

There the early evening afterglow tints the western horizon with twilight. Grace Thayer Bradley suggested that, were color translated into music, a trumpet fanfare, crashing symbols, and well-toned french horns would signal a complete orchestra's grand ensemble. "Rapidly the vivid shades softened; in the east filmy clouds were wrapped in that incomparable soft shell-pink they wear for those few moments just before the sun sinks from view."[154] The western symphonic harmony and unimaginable beauty seems intense.

> As soon as the top of the rim of the flaming disk sinks from sight, the ruby tinted water turns to cold grey; the marvelous colors which have held one gazing spell-bound, fade from the clouds; in sky and water have melted together in violet shadows, sharing one cloak against the chill of the night.[155]

The wilderness sanctuary provides unspoken testimony to strength and solace, and the growing trees seem representative for the Chicago clergyman.

> Every tree calls me to consider the secret of its beauty and strength, how it grew here in the wilds, responding to the influences of sun and air, of heat and cold, of dew and windstorm, seeming to find strength in battling with the elements, yielding neither to discouragement nor fear, holding its head high and with all its might growing into the best tree it can be in its environment.[156]

Towering pines, silent against a splendid horizon, symbolize the pastor, who, standing alone, learned from personal experience that moments of solitude nurture quiet courage and independent thought and that human greatness comes not from removing oneself from the world but in ministering graciously to man's spirit. Perspective for tomorrow comes from reflection.

> The leaves on the island are beginning to turn, the birches with golden hue and the maples with brilliant red. This morning I heard a blue-jay—always a sign of fall. Yesterday on the highway we saw a sleek, graceful deer, and in coming home from Tower late the other evening, where I had given an address, we saw a fine old black bear. The ducks are beginning to think of their southward journey, the days are growing shorter and the nights much cooler. The warblers have left! Yes, it's fall up here and our thoughts are about our church, its future and tomorrow![157]

PART TWO

Sermons
by The Reverend Dr. Preston Bradley

What Is Christianity?

What is Christianity? For nearly two thousand years, twenty centuries, philosophers, theologians, historians, and scientists have been attempting to answer that question. Obviously, it is not within the possibility of the time at my disposal this morning to do more than intimate my own personal interpretation of what Christianity is. The philosophers, present-day theological intellects, and masterminds of theology are still arguing among themselves what Christianity is.

In our city today, and lecturing here for a period of two or three weeks, is one of the great theologians of our time, Dr. Paul Tillich. I have had the opportunity of hearing Dr. Tillich, the distinguished and internationally known theologian, who is lecturing at present at the University of Chicago, and of reading his books. The probabilities are that his theological thinking is influencing more young men in the theological seminaries of the world than any other single mind.

Men like the great Rheinhold Niebuhr, men on both sides of the Atlantic, masterly men, are trying to answer the question. The scientists, because of the unprecedented development of space and man's effort to penetrate sidereal space, which he is successfully doing, are compelling a complete change of emphasis in the theological world. No longer are we an earth-centered cosmos. No longer is this earth the center of the universe. Consequently, any theological thinking which was limited by the areas of the physically known in the experiences of the thinker is no longer tenable. The mind of man must keep time and keep pace with the unfoldment of the cosmos, and to think of Christianity in terms of anthropomorphic concepts is to think of Christianity in terms of its man-made origins.

Now we have come to the greatest challenge that the mind

of man has ever faced: how to fit in the new concepts of science, space, distance, and conquest with the fundamental principles enunciated by the Galilean so long ago. The greatest challenge before Christianity today is the challenge of "catching up" with science. Science is compelling a complete reorientation of every basic philosophy identified as Christian. Therefore, when we ask the question today, "What is Christianity?" perhaps it is better for a moment or two, from my point of view, to say what Christianity is not. And it is easier, I think, to say what Christianity is not than to say what Christianity is.

Christianity, to me, is not a church—any church. I find no evidence whatever in sacred writ that Jesus ever intended to found a church; that He was ever interested in projecting His philosophy and spiritual sensitivity into any form of external organization. That was entirely the technique of the Apostle Paul. And in a very true historical sense we can say that Paul was the founder of Christianity and not Jesus. It was Paul who organized Christianity and not the Master. And there wasn't anything that even approximated the modern Christianity until the fourth century, more than three hundred years after Jesus had died! At the beginning of the Council of Nicea in 325 A.D., we find the beginning of institutionalized Christianity. Jesus knew nothing about it! He had no concept that His crystallization of faith in God and man should finally result in competitive ecclesiastical organizations, or that the world of Christianity would be divided into the tragedy of four hundred different kinds of Protestant churches, fourteen different kinds of Catholic churches, with a sprinkling of "fringe" creeds and faiths and beliefs scattered down through the years.

I hope I will not be misunderstood, but I am under the compulsion of stating only my own conviction; and I'm quite sure that even those who would most vitally disagree with me cannot help but respect that attitude. I think if Jesus, this simple, lovely heart, were to come back today and walk down the aisles of some of our great, majestic, and imposing churches and witness some of the spectacular ceremonies of Christianity, with the jewels and the silken garments, with all of the association and attachment that goes with the impressiveness of the spectacular—if Jesus were to come back today and attend some of these great spectacular evidences of ecclesiastical strength and power, I think He would say, "What is this all about? What is this all about—this pageantry, this wealth, these crosses of mine that are 'so high they part the stars'?" One church in our own city boasts of the fact, and it puts on its advertisement: "The Highest Cross in the City of Chicago!" I don't think that's a compliment—for the cross of this man dragged in the dirt. The cross of this man, Jesus, was so lowly and so heavy that He couldn't carry it Himself; and out of the mob that was following Him to the mountain, one helped Him carry His cross!

Ladies and gentlemen, the power of Christianity and the force of Christianity, to me, is when the principles of Christ are applied to the areas where men live. This great-hearted, kindly, simple carpenter's son wouldn't know what you were talking about if He listened to an argument in the churches about the difference between consubstantiation and transubstantiation! Do you know the difference? I question whether there are very many in the congregation or who are listening, except those who are trained in the niceties and the distinctions of theological thought, who could tell the difference; and yet, that difference between consubstantiation and transubstantiation has split the Christian Church wide open for centuries. And on one side and on the other intellectual disagreements go on and controversies continue about something that I don't think the Master would know anything about, and furthermore, about which I don't think He would care. I don't think He would care!

What is Christianity in this age? Christianity has a great uniqueness among all the religions that have arisen in the hearts of men—a great uniqueness—and that uniqueness is frequently forgotten: in all the other great religions of the world it is man seeking God; Christianity at its highest is God seeking man. That's its distinction: that there is a great operating, directed, creative, overpowering imperative in life that is constantly wooing man, that is saying to man, "Don't do that! Don't scar your soul with that! Don't be foolish!"—that is constantly pressing against the sensitive plate of the human heart and saying, "Don't! Don't!

I'm wooing you, wooing you into the highest and the best and the most beautiful! Don't be satisfied with barnyard morality! Don't be satisfied with the stupidity that there is a permanent enjoyment in sin!" Christianity presents God wooing man. That's its genius. That isn't true of Buddhism; it isn't true of Mohammedanism; it isn't true of Shintoism; it isn't true of Taoism; it isn't true of any religion the world has ever known. And the uniqueness of that appeal is found in the personality of this Galilean. That's the heart of it.

There are attitudes of worship that some people demand in which others find no compensation at all. Some love form, order, pageantry—all of it goes with the symbolism and the mysticism of Christianity. I grant all that, and I would be the very last to take from anyone's heart the compensation that comes from that type of worship. I would never do that, nor would I be guilty of it. But in this world Christianity is a minority religion; compared with the combined religions of the earth it is a very great minority religion. And when you believe as I do, it is the ethics of Jesus, the sacrifices of Jesus, and the spirit of Jesus which have magnetized all humanity with goodness; that is, the chief quality of Christianity is the spiritual emanation that grows out of the personality of the Galilean. It's not in form; it's not in creed; it's not in ceremony; it's not in ritual—these things all become sounding brass and tinkling cymbals if they cannot, and do not, apply to the life of man the redemptive philosophy and love of the Galilean, a love that is bigger than any church, that is more expansive than any creed.

No creed ever written is sufficiently inclusive to contain all the truth. Show me a creed, in this hour when a universe is being born, that has all the truth. It is nonexistent—in this hour. The passing of the old Newtonian physics has introduced values into the structure of society and the universe that the theologians of the twelfth and thirteenth centuries never even dreamed were in existence. Therefore, nothing can be validated now merely because it is old. Merely because a thing has worked is no longer any evidence that it will always work. We're in a new kind of a universe now, a new kind of a world. And the uniqueness of this

What Is Christianity?

Christianity in this modern world, to me, is to be found in a fundamental truth: that it is the only one of the religions of the world, which I know anything about, that's trying to woo the heart of man into dignity and greatness. That is why it has been the handmaiden of peace and freedom. That explains the Christianity of the founding fathers of freedom in the world—that, and that alone.

Christianity is the only religion that I know of—the only one—that loved man so much that the Galilean peasant was willing to die for man. Buddha didn't do that. Mohammed didn't do that. None of the religions of the world contained that element. Only the Galilean loved humanity so deeply, so completely, so sympathetically, that He said, "I'll die for you." And He did. That is the heart and the soul of Christianity, to me.

Do We Need Another Reformation?

Four hundred and twenty-five years ago tomorrow—nearly five hundred years ago tomorrow—on All Saints' Eve, Martin Luther nailed on the castle church door in Wittenberg, Germany, ninety-five expressions of disapproval of the church of which he was a priest. Those ninety-five manifestations of intellectual courage and of moral stamina on the part of Martin Luther have influenced all subsequent theology and all subsequent ecclesiastical history.

On this Sunday the whole Protestant world is giving emphasis to the results, as they interpret them, of that great moment. It was not the beginning of the historical Reformation, for other personalities had preceded Luther in laying the foundation of the spirit of the Reformation; but preceding this was an historical episode of as great a significance to the cultural and educational world as the action of Luther was to the religious and theological world: the great epic of history known as the Renaissance.

The Renaissance preceded the Reformation, and the Renaissance was the reformation of the European intellect. And in the centuries in which the mind of man had been held in the bondage and slavery of ignorance and illiteracy—when the scientists, and science, were repudiated, and any advance in the world of intellectuality which seemed to dispute the sovereignty of the supernatural was held a prisoner—we had those tragic ages called the Dark Ages, which were dark because the mind of man was imprisoned. Any age is a Dark Age that attempts to stifle the thinking of man. Any church or any religion needs a Reformation that seeks to circumscribe with limitation the intellectual assault of man upon the mystery of the universe or the identity and reality of God. There is no more despicable power in the world than the power that seeks to control the mind and the heart of man. No matter whether you call it a church, a creed, a theology, or whatever you call it, it belongs in the category of resistance and retrogression.

The Renaissance was the reformation of the European intellect. The intellect of man was released so that without fear it could continue the necessary investigation and evaluation which does not make a smaller God but creates a larger God. No microscope yet was ever an enemy of religious truth; no telescope was ever an enemy of religious truth; no laboratory was ever truly in conflict with the theological rostrum. Wherever truth is investigated, wherever truth is revealed, and wherever truth is discovered, there is the handmaiden of true religion. There is no religion higher than truth; there *can be* no religion higher than truth. Truth is the ultimate expression of man's persistency to find affinity with the universe of which he is a part. And this quest of the intellect of man to continue his study, his hope, and his thought, unrestricted by creed or ecclesiasticism, whether Roman Catholic or Protestant, is one of the earmarks of religious progress. No institution, no church, no creed, no dogma has ever been able to stifle the questing spirit of man. And when any church, no matter what its designation, no matter what its place or its historic position, seeks to set a limitation over the mind of man, that church is fundamentally antagonistic to religion at its highest and at its best. Therefore, when we study the principles of the Renaissance, we find it the prelude to the Reformation; and the Reformation was nothing more or less than the renaissance of European morality. Just as the Renaissance was the reformation of the European intellect, so the Reformation was the renaissance of European morality. And men recaptured the capacity to think fearlessly for himself and to face the future unafraid, knowing that truth was never the enemy of his religion and that superstition and fear are never the earmarks of religious reality. And the great struggle of the ages of man to be free started.

Now, when I ask the question this morning, "Do we need another Reformation?" my answer is immediately, strongly, and firmly, "Yes!" For we find ourselves today in the same category, throughout much of the religious world, that the religious world possessed five hundred years ago. When any ecclesiastical institution which grows out of the transforming beauty of freedom will itself become guilty of assuming the technique which it sought, through reformation, to completely destroy, then there is need for another Reformation. And many of the ecclesiastical institutions today in the world of Christendom are guilty—equally guilty— of the same attitude toward truth that inspired the Reformation five hundred years ago. For any church that closes the door, or announces through a creed that here is all the truth there is—that unless you conform to what we think theologically you are wrong and doomed and damned—is in need of a Reformation. You can call it Roman Catholicism, or you can call it Lutheranism, or you can call it Unitarianism, or you can call it any other kind of "ism" you please. But when any ecclesiastical body seeks to limit the mind of man and write a creed or a dogma and present it to the world and say, "This is all there is to religious truth; there is no more; and unless you conform to what we believe you are lost and doomed and damned"; when the world of Christendom reaches the point where it attempts to express finality of truth and of Christian beauty in the terms of a man-made creed—for all of the creeds were written by men, and the great creeds of the Church everywhere were creeds that were the creation of their age and of their mentality—then that church is in need of a Reformation. The great Apostles' Creed, which is recited by the millions in Christendom today, no Apostle ever saw; no Apostle ever heard;

no Apostle ever wrote. And these creeds—the Nicene Creed, the Creed of Athanasius, the Apostles' Creed, and all the creeds of Christendom today—are the products of man's effort to state theologically the conception of final truth in religion.

The greatest truth of Protestantism is not in its antagonism to Roman Catholicism or in the bickering of people between creeds, churches, and religions. The greatest religion in the world is the religion to be free. Freedom was the very spirit of Christ; freedom was the very essence of the Christian gospel; freedom was the very basic and fundamental concept of the mentality and spiritual beauty of the Master himself. And anyone who seeks to limit that cannot, by any classification, be accepted as the final authority in religion.

I believe that we have not yet even crossed the threshold of the full revelation of religious truth.

I believe there will be new religious leaders come to every culture of the world, of every race and every country.

I believe that there will be an increase of man's conception of his relationship to God that will startle all the creeds and startle all the churches.

I believe in the new Reformation.

In that Reformation so long ago, there was a man of courage, a man of intellectual candor, a man of moral heroism who stood fearlessly and in great danger. One who stands opposed to the status quo is always in great danger. It is easier and it is safer to think with the crowd; it is easier and more respectable to go with the multitude; it is easier to follow the line of least resistance; it is easier to have the acclaim of society. But he is great who dares face the challenge of solitude and loneliness but be on good terms with his own conscience. The greatest statement that Martin Luther ever made—greater than any contribution which he made to the subsequent religious thinking of the world—the greatest thing that Martin Luther ever said on this Reformation Sunday was when he stood, almost alone, and faced every power against him. And standing there quietly, he said, "Here I stand. I can do nothing else."

That is the Reformation we need today. We need a Reformation everywhere in the realm of individual and heroic, intellectual and spiritual, courage. Let us experience in our hearts and minds that kind of a Reformation, and I guarantee that we will remake the world in another ten years. Let the tyranny everywhere cease: the tyranny of ecclesiastical limitation, the tragedy of what is taking place in Wisconsin today, when, in this century—the last half of the twentieth century—we can observe in the name of the Reformation spirit, the trying of young men in the pulpit for heresy who have the courage to think for themselves, who have the courage to stand up and say, "Here I stand. I can do no other."

On this Reformation day I welcome the spirit of Martin Luther; I welcome the spirit of St. Francis of Assisi. You are not most Protestant when you are most anti-Catholic; you are best Christian when you see the values of both and, with intellectual and spiritual heroism, stand up, even if you stand alone. That day of the new Reformation is about to dawn. People are growing tired of the tyranny of quasi-educated spiritual leaders who are afraid of science, afraid of the fundamental processes of reason, and who are so fearful for their theology that they would defend it with the instrument of ignorance. That day is passing—thank God!

Is God Dead?

I wish I had almost a lifetime to talk about our theme this morning—"Is God Dead?" Why the question at all?

There has arisen in the theological thought of the world an attitude toward the reality of God unlike any other in the history of human thought. The interesting paradox is that the great professors of theology in many of the seminaries of the world—certainly in Europe, and also on this side of the Atlantic—are beginning a theological penetration and an analysis of God unprecedented in the history of human thought. Many of them have become so completely radical in the presentation of their concept that God has passed out of the picture. Articles are appearing entitled, "Is God Dead?" The newspapermen are holding great conferences and dialogues on theology. The better magazines and newspapers are giving great attention to this problem of God; and I haven't the time to exhaust all of the many, many reactions which I have as an individual.

I make no pretense of being a profound theologian. Much of their phraseology is so involved for me that I find it very difficult to follow them in their logical processes of developing ideas. I am concerned with the reality of something which means God to me. I would be the first to recognize that the old concepts of God are dying; that they ought to die; that they have been an interference with the experiential relationship to the reality of God. For God is something to be experienced and not to be argued. One will never sense nearness to reality of the cosmos merely through arguments. It can only come through experience. The reality of God is an experiential performance—not merely an intellectual theory. It is based upon experience. And my conclusions that I make—and I must make my conclusions at the very beginning of the sermon—are such that I think, unless I am being self-deceived, are based on the reality of experience.

The old anthropomorphic conception of God is dying, and, as I said a moment ago, it ought to die. Man, an incurably religious institution, has been attempting for probably several hundred millions of years to find an answer to the mystery of his own identity. That is the basis of all religion. It is based in mystery, and until we recognize the quality of the mystery we are going to be confused in our concept of the God idea. The old anthropomorphic God was the creation of man. Man has been attempting through his mentality to define God. Man has been making an effort to crystallize God into a formula, and he has been saying God is this and God is that. That God who "walked in the cool of the garden" is an anthropomorphic God. The God who dwelt like the gods on Mt. Olympus is an anthropomorphic conception of God.

But the mind of man through the ages has had no other norm by which to determine the quality and the character of the infinite except that of his own creation. Man has been creating a concept of God himself, forgetting that God created man. Man has been creating God, with the result that our various intellectual concepts of God are abroad everywhere in our present-day theology and in our philosophy of religion. We are praying to norms of our own creation: a God who is a jealous God, an angry God; a God who could be satisfied by the cruel murder of an innocent man; a God who would kill little children because they made fun or made light of some old man, as you will find recorded in the Old Testament; a God who was the God Jehovah, a tribal God. How can we think of the immensity of the reality of God as being a Jehovah who belongs to one tribe or one group of men?

One of the most interesting evolutions in the whole realm of theology centers around this idea of God—the God of the early days of the Old Testament, down through the thousand years between the Old Testament and the New, until we come to the God that shows the impregnation of the philosophy of Greece. For we must never forget that Paul, from whom we read this morning in the scripture reading, gave one of the greatest theological concepts of God that the world has ever had, and he gave it at Athens, on Mars Hill. The greatest thrill I had in some respects on our recent journeys was in standing on Mars Hill in Athens, Greece. As we stood there looking out over the Acropolis, with its great, classic structure, the Parthenon, I heard again the great words of the Apostle Paul, probably the most philosophic mind which Christianity has ever produced. And I heard him say, "He whom ye ignorantly worship, I announce unto you."

The infiltration of Greek theology into the Christian-Hebraic, Christian tradition of theology of the concept of God is affirmed in the highest manifestation of the sublime principle of God that has ever been revealed to man, in the life and personality and teaching and beauty of the Christ. For it remained for Him, in His concept of God, to go beyond the little man-made structure of human history—the God who was but a reflection of ourselves, the man-made God, capable of all the passions and the anger and the cruelty and the persecution and the hate of the human heart—a God of vengeance, who brought floods, wars, and all the rest of the tragic angles of history. I have never accepted that interpretation of God. God doesn't create wars; He does not create floods; He does not afflict the innocent.

God's spirit is not in conspiracy against the highest concept of life that the human heart could possibly know. Where do we have to go to find the reality of God—the God that is not dead? The theologians are dealing with dead gods and dead issues. They belong in the same category as the man who refers to God as "the man upstairs." That wounds me; it wounds me through and through when I hear anyone refer to "the man upstairs." That is the concept of God which is dying, and that is the concept of God which ought to die, because it is as far removed from the creative, continuing impulses of the cosmos—as we see life manifested everywhere—as anything could possibly be.

Where do we have to go to find the concept of God that is not dying, that never will die—the great concept of Professor Paul Tillich? This evening I am going to appear at 9 o'clock on the television program "I See Chicago" in "The World Revolution in Religion." They have asked me to speak, surrounded by a group of men whose theological concepts are entirely different from my own; but I have consented to appear and will appear on that program, together with Dr. Tillich, though his body now is dust and his brain is in a glass jar at the University of Chicago Medical Center. The mind still lives; that is the God projection, the eternity of infinite truth. Nothing can ever happen to that. That is a part of the structure of the cosmos of which we are a part.

Who can define God? There never has been a definition of God ever written. God never sat for His photograph; and these people who say they can define God are tragic individuals, not only in the inferiority of their mentality, but also in the inferiority of their comprehension of God, and they are to be pitied.

God cannot be defined. No creed was ever yet written that could define Him. You can't define the infinite. You have no physical brain capacity—not any one of us has—to comprehend infinity. No one knows how long eternity is. There is no concept in the physical structure of a brain cell that could possibly measure infinity. You can't measure it; in that sense you can't measure God. God must be experienced: the reality of divine love and divine truth, the spiritual essence of life itself, for what dear, blessed Dr. Tillich calls "the ground of our being." But you can't define it; you can't put it into words; you can't put it into a mathematical formula.

There is no conflict between true science and true religion—none whatever. One deals with the eternal *effactu;* the other deals with the eternally growing, developing and changing. And the highest idea of God that man ever had was the idea that came from the lips of the Master Teacher of Galilee. And when I think of what has arisen in His name—the superstitions and the fears; the creeds and the infinite variety of denominations; all the wrangling and the fighting and the quarreling; "I am right, you are wrong"; "This is the only true church; believe this church or you are damned"—what has God, the eternal spirit, to do with all that childishness? Nothing! Not a thing!

Jesus gave us the answer: "God is love." That's the only definition known of God, the only thing the Bible tells us God is. God is love. And when, in our association with each other, in our sense of responsibility to life, we reflect that love, then I know the presence of God; then it becomes an experience and not a theory. Only those who have have experienced the reality of divine truth can speak with authority of the character and meaning of God. The rest, who judge it all by human standards and human methods and human means, never can comprehend the reality of the divine, until they cleanse their minds from the pettiness of mundane, earthly things.

> "I know not where his islands
> Lift their fronded palms in air;
> I only know I cannot drift
> Beyond his loving care."

Space-Age Religion

When the historian of the year 5000—and there will be a year 5000—looks back upon this age in which you and I live, I sometimes speculate a little bit in my own mind as to whether he will be able to find a phrase which will, with accuracy and inclusiveness, describe the age in which you and I live. We know that the historians of the past have such phrases and have used them to describe certain segments of human history. By way of example, when I use the phrase "the Golden Age of Greece," every person who knows classical history at all knows what that phrase describes. "The Golden Age of Greece." We see the chisel in the hands of Phidias; we listen to the philosophic dissertation of one of the seven greatest minds of all time, the mind of Socrates; we listen to Plato and hear again the plays of Aristophanes and the poems of Theocritus.

We know, when we come across the phrase "the Golden Age of Greece," what that phrase means. And the probabilities are that the historian of the year 5000, when the evolutionary processes of science and religion have had their way in the next forty centuries, will look back upon this age and will find such a phrase. It will not be as long as the phrase "the Golden Age of Greece," but I think probably he will use only four words to describe the age: "the Age of Space."

This is the age in which man is continually outlining larger areas of thought; this is the age where the horizons are being lifted; this is the age when the limitations of the past are being removed; this is an age when religion is being compelled, under the unquestionable advance of knowledge of the cosmos, to rethink every one of its traditional values; this is an age when the mind of man is pushing out and out and out and out, until the barriers that he was compelled to face in much of his history are being eliminated.

Space-age religion! There is no segment of our civilization that can escape this influence. It is occurring in every area. It is occurring in education, and the educators are being compelled to readjust and realign their whole emphasis in the area of education —space-age education. The old, traditional emphasis in the area are being dissipated by the necessities of the present and the consequences of this present. The same is true in business; business is being compelled in this kind of an age to readjust and to reevaluate much of its technique of the old competitive days of

Space-Age Religion

industry. That is disappearing and disappearing rapidly. It is true in the realm of government; governments of the world everywhere are being compelled to readjust and reevaluate some of the fundamental principles upon which all government is based.

Now we come specifically to the question of religion. What is going to happen, and what is happening, to religion in this age, this space age? Religion cannot escape the influence of this spatial development. Any religion that, like the ostrich, seems to put its head into the sand and refuses to admit that which vision and intelligence reveal is a dying religion. That religion will decay, will disappear, will dissipate. When religion does not open its mind and its heart to the infiltrations of the new significance of this space age, that religion, no matter how old it is, will disappear. For the real validity of religion does not depend on its antiquity, but it does depend upon what it is doing to meet the problems of human society and the problems of our scientific age. The mere fact that it is old is not enough. The mere fact that it has been in the world for fifty or sixty centuries is not enough. The mere fact that a thing has lasted is not conclusive evidence that it will be continuous. It is only as education and government and religion come to terms with the enlarged cosmos of which we are all a part that we see the reality of divine creation.

God has not yet completed His act of creation. He is not a fiat God, but a dynamic God. There is no absolutism or finality to the processes of the cosmos. Man has not yet even crossed the threshold; he has hardly got his foot over the step into the unknown cosmos of reality. How foolish it is to hold onto a religious interpretation that agrees with the concept of religious thought that the earth is held on the back of a turtle, or that it was created in seven days (like the seven days that you and I know), or that God had confined His whole energy to one little planet in the cosmos, where there are a million million suns as great as ours and where there are indescribable and inconceivable solids floating through infinity! When the mind of man comes face to face with the colossal evidence of creativeness and of the divine intelligence which must be behind the creativeness, then the little pettiness of superstitions and fears in his religion must disappear if he is to survive; then his little bigotries, his devotion to man-made creeds, his attention to the little patterns that have accumulated through the centuries, all become incompetent and impotent to face the realities of a space age.

Now, can religion come face to face with this age? I say to you it can. It does not mean the end of religion; it means the increase of the vitality of true religion; it means that this will be the elimination of the petty smallness of man's mind, conditioned by his superstitions and his fears. It will be the awakening of his intelligence and his heart, until he will eliminate poverty, disease, sin, economic distortions, industrial inequities, and the collapse of morality in high places. A religion that does not, in this space age, have something to say about these things now and here in the light of that divine intelligence is a religion that may have the throngs, the crowds, and the emotions of the present hour, while a few minority minds and hearts see vividly the truth, but that religion will disappear. And the great eternal truths of religion in the reality of God will be revealed, for God is in the process of revelation. The last Bible has not been written. The Bibles are still being written. The highest achievement of the human personality has not been met: there are areas of art and music, there are areas of culture and beauty, that man has yet to explore. We are only on the threshold; and to think that what's happening is decadent is, in my humble opinion, impossible.

Do you remember the story—it's a very familiar story—of Br'er Fox and Br'er Rabbit in the briar patch? Do you remember that? When a world is in the briar patch and many of our lives are in the briar patch, when we are being hurt and scarred and people are having difficult times—it was in just such an hour that religion was born. Judaism came out of exile. It was the basis of the synagogue and the temple. And it happened not in the days of the ease and triumph of Zion; it was in the days when they met together in the tragedy of the exile. That was the birth of Judaism. Christianity did not come in an era of ease and affluence when the whole world's society, with open arms, was receiving the man of Galilee. No! It came when a great empire was dissolving in the tragedies of disunity and disorganization. And upon the wrecks of that empire came a sweet, spirited youth from Galilee. And it was born in a briar patch.

This is the hour for the highest demonstration of eternal religious truth and the magnificent creativeness of the divine mind. It was in such an hour that religion and its power were born. And it is in such an hour that the condition generates in us a response to that power. Spage-age religion! May religion occupy space! And now, may the presence of that divine mind be in each of our hearts; may it have breadth and scope and depth; may it be sensitive to suffering and injustice and, above all, in the briar patches of life may we have the courage to meet life.

The Celebration of Life

There are approximately eight hundred million Christians on this earth. Eight hundred million! Today most of them are filling the churches and the cathedrals, the great places around the earth, and the one song that is upon their lips is "Christ is Risen." It will sound from the altars and the pulpits of Christendom around the world. Following the mandate of my own interpretation and thinking, I cannot help observing something that might be construed as a negative approach to this idea. The one day in which we should not be negative is this day, but I cannot help it and be honest with myself. Eight hundred million throats are shouting, "Christ is Risen!" I ask a question: Is it true?

I am not thinking or speaking in regard to any theological interpretation of Christ. I have long since ceased to be interested in the theological arguments about Him. They do not command my energy, intellectual or physical. I am not concerned with the infinite variety of creeds which have been written about Him down through the ages. That doesn't concern me. I am not concerned with the difference between transubstantiation and consubstantiation. I question whether there is anyone except a theologically trained individual who knows the difference between transubstantiation and consubstantiation. But that difference separated the Christian church for fifteen hundred years and still separates into theological areas the Christian church of today. That is a problem which most members of the Christian church have no comprehension about whatever. Then when Christendom celebrates, popes and bishops and priests and pastors and ministers have a feeling of exaltation: "Christ is Risen!"

The question I am asking as I stand at my little window of the world and look out upon the passing pageantry of our modern life is "Do you mean it?" With violence raising its ghastly head in many areas of the life of the world, I do not need to reiterate or repeat the contemporary agony that we have been experiencing. I never expected when I came to this pulpit that only those two wonderful years, 1912 to 1914, would be years when not a shot was fired anywhere in the world. Those first two years in this pulpit were years of peace for mankind. And if anyone had told me then that I would ever live to see the agony of the world which I am experiencing now, I wouldn't have believed them. I would have ridiculed their judgment and would not have accepted it. And then one day, when I was in Europe, there dropped out of a clear sky a flash of lightning; and that flash of lightning lit afire every powder magazine of the world. And it is still flashing.

So I have lived through two major wars, two minor conflicts, and the present world tragedy of my country and my world. And during all these years, they have shouted from the pulpits and the churches and the choir lofts of America, "Christ is Risen!" Then on Monday morning they have returned to the marts of trade as a factor in the economy of a society that has created those dastardly things called "the ghetto" and "the slum." With the protection and security of society on the outside, the profiteer bargains with the souls of men, and battles plague the ghettos and the slums of America. But they sing, "Christ is Risen."

This is no hour for the coward, the compromiser, or the equivocater. Do you mean Christ is risen, you and the hierarchy of Christendom who have it all in your hands and have organized countless conflicting contingencies? You are all singing today, at your flower-bedecked altars, "Christ is Risen." So I ask the question, "Do you mean it?" I ask you, "Are you sincere?" That's a tremendous indictment to raise against anyone, but I ask you. Fourteen different kinds of Catholics in the world and four hundred different branches of Protestantism are divided into various ecclesiastical and church groups, disagreeing on the kind of water to be used in baptism; arguing about the various means of grace; fighting and quarreling in theological fear. I ask you various Christians who have been singing that Christ is risen, "Do you mean it? Do you really mean it?"

Well, the conclusion of the matter is, you had better mean it. You had better take this Christ whom you are extolling and magnifying in your acts of worship and let Him live in your life. What would happen if eight hundred million people in the world this morning really meant it?

This young Nazarene, this dreamer, this poet, only had three years of public ministry; and He cannot be impeached in one single ethical pronouncement. If He could come back some Sunday morning and walk down the aisles of the churches—with the quarrels, the criticisms, the attacks, the innuendoes, and the ecclesiastical jealousies—I think He would say, "What's all this about? What are they doing to me? I don't know anything about your arguments and your theological controversies. I don't know what you are talking about when you talk about God being dead. I once thought that God had forsaken me when I hung upon a cross, but He hadn't. I don't know what you are talking about. What's this all about?"

Oh, my friends, in the compulsion of this moment, I tremble with a sense of responsibility. I know that He has the answer. I have no doubts about that. I know He has the way. He said once, "I am the way." That's true. Where did we get off the way? What happened to our fine intellects that can make a parking space of the sky, chart the bottom of the sea, press a button and light a continent, whisper around the world, and annihilate oceans and mountains creating one world for mankind? What happened?

We have been singing "Christ is Risen." Are you sure? What are you doing, what am I doing, with the risen Christ? Are we putting His way into execution? Are we sacrificing for the pilgrimage to the eternal? Christ is risen! Yes! When we do away with slums, racial hatred, war, and all the other damnable monstrosities that are bringing wrack and ruin to human society. Then you can sing "Christ is Risen," when you put into operation the things He stood for. Until you do that, your religion is sounding brass and a tinkling cymbal. Now we are being challenged, and we must meet the challenge as never before. And if we do, then the indestructibility of good, truth, and beauty will be proven. That is the real spirit of the Resurrection.

Easter says you can't kill goodness; you can't kill beauty; you can't kill honor. Easter is the example of the fundamental rectitude of God. The Nazarene's enemies said, "We got rid of this fanatical Jew. We have killed him." Easter says, "You can't kill goodness and truth and beauty." And if we can get that into our hearts and into our souls, we will have a different world. We will have a better world. Your light will shine. Make it shine! Be that kind of personality that, when you come around, you bring light.

Newspaper row in Boston: it was dark and gloomy one afternoon, with fog blowing in from the bay. A newspaper reporter sat at his typewriter in the composing room, and he was just improvising. He looked out. And it was dark and raining. But he went back to his typewriter and wrote, "Yes, it is dark and foggy and rainy today. But Phillips Brooks just passed by, and the sun shines."

Faith is passing by, and the sun shines. Live that kind of life, and man will find his way back again to dignity, to greatness, and to peace.

They Call It Progress

Forty-four years ago this very day, fifty-four men, including myself, sat down at a table in the Chicago Club and organized the Izaak Walton League of America. Last night we had a Founders' Day Dinner in the Blackstone Hotel. There are only three of us living of the group who organized the League forty-four years ago this very day: two others and myself. I was the only charter member present last night.

It is events of this character that inspire me to continue what I have emphasized all my life: that there is something called progress; that in spite of all the obstacles, failures, setbacks, disappointments, and disillusionments we have in our society, there is, deep down underneath, something that is saying to man, "Don't give up." No matter how many wars, how much trouble, racial hatred, and despair we have, there is something that says, "Don't give up." Now, that is the basis of all progress. Macauley said in his great essay on civilization that man and civilization embody the principles of progress. And he is right. The principle of progress is there, and it has never been completely eliminated from the human motivation. Never. You will always find in every church, society, government, and business the individual who—when things are the blackest and failure seems to be impending—says, "Don't let go." Always somebody comes with a word of encouragement or with an action which solves the problem.

Now, they are constantly telling me two things as I travel about the world. I have heard them around the world, on both sides of the Atlantic. I never get into a taxicab that I don't get into conversation with the driver. It may not be too important, but I have learned something. And they are telling me two things these days. The first thing is, "Man has always fought and always will. There has always been war, and there will always be war." I had a man tell me that this week. "Why," he said, "Dr. Bradley, with your idealism, you are just barking down a rain barrel. Don't you know that man has always fought and always will?"

And the second thing they are telling me every day is that history always repeats itself. Now, I am frank to say to you that I don't believe either one of those things, and I would debate them or challenge them with any authority in their respective fields. I don't accept the theory at all that because man has been fighting all of these centuries he is always going to fight —that he is never going to find the way of peace. And there are many distinguishing historical instances that would justify that position. You would naturally assume, as you turn the pages of history down through the ages, that when man can no longer settle his problems by reason, by conference, by ideas, he will fight. That has been the history of civilization. That doesn't mean to me that he will always use that technique. Someday he is going to grow wise and courageous enough to get rid of this useless institution called war; for the world and the country never had a war that didn't create bigger problems than it tried to solve. War creates problems; it doesn't solve them. And we are still facing problems that have come from every war this country ever had. But to believe that it is inevitable I repudiate with my whole soul and in spite of my intellectual limitations, which are many. But I repudiate that fallacy of history.

Man was designed for something great. The mere fact that you are you and I am I is conclusive evidence to you and to me that there is an importance to human personality, that anything which disturbs that personality is basically an enemy of the future. One of these centuries man is going to find the better way. He will never let that motivation perish. There will come in the darkest hour an artist, a poet, a soul, a sensitive life, and he will see the highway that leads to the full fruition of the human personality. And he will be opposed to anything that destroys human personality. I believe that is inherently a part of the human spirit.

Neither do I believe the second thing—that history repeats itself. History is spherical, and there are moments in the history of man when the sphere almost coincides with the previous era—but it never quite reaches it. Man is never the same in his cyclical history. There isn't a person in this congregation this morning who will be the same person when he goes out as he was when he came in. Man is in a state of fluctuation. We are actually at the mercy of every influence that touches the aura of personality; and it does something to you, and it does something to me.

If history repeats itself, how much better it would have been if God, the creator of man, had never created him. Why, O God —and I sometimes feel like saying it to Him directly—why did You not just go on enjoying the beauty of Your own creation, enjoying the sublimity of the world You made: the mountains, the sunset, the moonlit nights, the glory of the dawn, the majesty of noonday? God, why did You not just enjoy Your own creation and leave man out of it? Why did You create man at all if he is to be doomed and damned, that the best he can do in every generation is to take the youth, who have every right to live, and slaughter them? Why did You create man if war is indispensable and history repeats itself? Why didn't You go on enjoying the majesty and beauty of Your creation, God, and leave man out, if You have trapped him and caught him in a circle or in a repetition of history?

I don't believe history repeats itself. I think that in every epoch, when man is through with it, he is a little bit higher. Somewhere his finer sensitivity has been aroused. Somewhere there is a better way than racial hatreds, which deprive the people of opportunity because of their color, or organizing institutions to fight another religion. These are the things that will breed murder on the streets and looting on the highways. So man asks himself, "Why can't I find a better way? Why can't we develop a better technique? Why can't we get rid of this ghastly, awful, gnawing hate that destroys everything it touches and agonizes every heart which hates?"

Man is stabbed with the eternal. There is a spirit of God in his heart that will not let him go. God turned him loose with a free will, and He said, "Man, you decide. I have given you intellect; I have given you the ability, all the advancement in science." We know more about the human body than we have ever known, and we are going to know more. Man can live longer than he has ever lived in the whole history of civilization. All these facts are realities. Now, man, why not use this same intellect; why not regulate these same emotions; why not control these ghastly dispositions that ripen into hate and murder? Why not build a foundation for a better world? That's the challenge in the human heart, and as long as that challenge exists there will be progress. As long as man dreams, there will be progress. As long as the poet sings, the artist paints, and the dramatist portrays, there will be progress. Something in the soul of man marches on toward the light and toward the dawn.

A little girl, walking with her mother after the rain, saw a puddle in which some oil was mixed with the water. You have all seen that iridescent light. And the little girl looked at that light in the puddle and said to her mother, "There is a rainbow gone to smash." As long as man keeps his rainbow from smashing, man will march onto the highway of peace.

Red or Dead?

Sixteen years ago on this very night I was on a train bound for the Pacific Coast. Accompanying me were some of the members of the United States delegation which had been appointed for the United Nations Charter Convention: Mr. Harold Stassen, who at the time was very much in the public eye; Senator Vandenberg of the state of Michigan; and many other representatives of this nation. It was a special train. The Secretary of State had appointed me an advisor to the State Department for the convention. I shall never forget the experience. I have followed, as closely and as carefully as I could, the sixteen intervening years in the life of the United Nations Organization.

I haven't time this morning to give you all the ramifications or most of the reactions which are in my heart today as I stand on this Sunday morning in our beloved pulpit sixteen years later. Democracies are always late. They always have been late, largely because in making decisions on what a democracy must do there are many different people who must be consulted and considered. That is not true with dictatorship. Dictatorship can act quickly and effectively. Democracies must take the slower process of consulting and of considering various points of view and various political loyalties. In a way it is one of the tragedies of democracy, as modern world history easily affirms. I happen to be one of those who believe that Mussolini could have been stopped in Ethiopia without the danger of a world war. If Mussolini had been stopped in Ethiopia, the whole history of the world would have been different, but the great democratic nations of the world—Britain, France and the United States—felt that it might jeopardize world peace if we stood up at that hour against Mussolini. It should have been done. Democracy was late. I happen to believe that we could have stopped Japan in Manchuria. Japan, without any steel, without any coal, was not prepared to make a military attack. And if the democratic nations of the world had stood up when Japan went into Manchuria, the whole of the world's history might have been changed. I happen to believe that democracy should have stood up when Hitler went into the Ruhr Valley. He was parading papier-mâché tanks in the streets of Berlin, trying to convince the people of his invincible power; he was shouting from the housetops, telling multitudes of people of his strength; he was making threats. But the democratic world was silent when Hitler went into the Ruhr Valley, and the rest is history.

I think we are reaching, at this moment in the history of our own country and our civilization, the kind of hesitancy which creates a universal fear in the hearts of people that they are to be suddenly wiped out and which is driving people to burrow like rabbits or moles in the earth in something called "shelters for fallout protection"; where the people are fearful something is going to annihilate them and wipe them out. It is creating an American psychology of danger that is doing something to the traditional stability and independent action of the American people.

On this day in which we observe the sixteenth anniversary of those nations which I saw sign this charter in the Opera House at San Francisco, we must look again at our problems. I think that the critical moment in which we find ourselves could be successfully met if we stood up again and spoke out without fear or trembling against every ideology that would destroy and mutilate the historic power of democracy.

This is the hour for greatness. This is the hour to cleanse our minds of every remnant of thought of total annihilation. This is the hour to do what is always effective when you're dealing with bullies. Khrushchev is the world's number one bully. He talks out of both sides of his mouth; one moment it is a threat of annihilation for the world, and the next moment it is a phrase calling for peace and brotherhood—all of which indicates to every student of the human personality that we are dealing with a psychopath. For in him we find the psychopathic character and the qualities of one who is pure bully and pure braggadocio. You never met a bully in your life who wasn't a coward. He talks loud, screams, and shouts; and when you call his bluff he seeks refuge and disappears.

I think the time has arrived when we should call Khrushchev's bluff. What has the democratic world to apologize for? What have we to be hesitant about? Why is America trembling and fearful? Why has this man created such a psychological atmosphere as has settled down upon all the world? Let him continue, and sooner or later—and I think it will be sooner—he will make the fatal blunder. He has indicated the quality of fatality in his last threat to explode a fifty-megaton bomb. I do not think a fifty-megaton bomb ever will be exploded, although *he* may do some unprecedented exploding. This belief of mine is determined by the fact that the neutral and noncommitted nations of the world have spoken out, and already in the last twenty-four hours there are reverberations from a large percentage of those whom Mr. Khrushchev feels are friendly to him. A friendship inspired by fear! And any friendship inspired by fear is a friendship that cannot endure. Friendships are not made through fear. Do you think that his so-called allies and friends are going to stick by him should he cover them with devastating fallout? Their admiration would turn to contempt. Protests are now being formulated, and they will be increasingly formulated, on the part of the very people, the very nations, and the very groups that Mr. Khrushchev is depending on in this hour. And Mr. Khrushchev and the Kremlin—the twelve men who control the policies of the people—will awaken some morning to the realization that will be the beginning of the end for the tyranny of the Soviet Union, and this will happen without war. I say this quite dogmatically.

You will remember these words in five or ten years—long after the voice which speaks them is silenced—but you will remember these words: *there will never be another world war.* There will be a series of localized conflicts and irritations. The young man of twenty in this congregation this morning will never, never know a world free from conflict and consternation. That world is here. The world that I knew in my youth has completely disappeared. I shall never know that kind of a world again. But in the presence of all this I have no hesitancy in saying to you—and I realize full well the responsibility of saying it—I am not afraid. Mr. Khrushchev does not have me buffaloed or in a corner.

I believe the time has arrived for a restoration and a renaissance of something of that spirit that wrote the Constitution of the United States and the Declaration of Independence. I wish we had men in the United States Senate and in the Congress who would say now, "Give me liberty or give me death," when people are obsessed with the slogan "Red or Dead." I tell you I shall never be Red; but I shall never be dead, destroyed by the militarism of a madman and a psychopath. The American people have been inspired by press and radio and by commentators to think they should burrow into the earth and build fallout shelters, until people are worried and frightened. That, to me, has in the background more than a suspicion of profit and dollars. I read an ad just the other day which said, "We will build you a fallout shelter and finance you over a five-year period!" Is there anything more incongruous, more ridiculous, than that? I'm not going to enter a fallout shelter!

I'm never going to enter a fallout shelter. I'm not going to be swayed by the emotionalisms of people who have selfish interests involved. I am not concerned, not at all. And furthermore, may I say I wouldn't want to live in this blessed country of mine should this tragedy happen to my own life or the life of my family. I wouldn't want to come out of a hole in the earth to a scorched nation, to a land that will not grow any grain or fruit for a hundred years due to the impregnation of poison. I don't want to live unless my friends can live with me—all of you. I don't want to live and have any other American die. I want to live with you—all of you. I don't want even the animals to suffer this tragedy. I don't want my country to get to the low ebb of moral sensitivity whereby selfish survival becomes more important than community survival. If I were the only person to come out of a fallout shelter in the city of Chicago if this disaster happened, I wouldn't want to live one hour.

My friends, let's get our values straight. Let's have a renaissance of something that's rapidly disappearing: old-fashioned courage. Let's not live in a world where we think evil is stronger than good and evil men are stronger than good men. I see no evidence that God has retired; I see no evidence that God has resigned—not one single bit of evidence. I see God weeping and pleading for a great renaissance of the same kind of courage that we heard in the lesson this morning. This is the psychology that ought to settle down upon the American people: every dictator finally meets his Waterloo.

Call the roll of history. Genghis Kahn, who held all of China, all of Asia in his hands—what happened to him? Call the roll of Napoleon. I stood at his tomb the other day in the city of Paris and looked down upon that tomb. Call the roll of Napoleon and see him standing a prisoner on a British frigate and watching the shores of his beloved France fade away into the fog of an unrealized ambition. Come with me to that little city in Italy where I stood on the very spot where Mussolini died, hanging by his heels with filth and water running out of his nostrils, while the people kicked at him and spit at him—the same people who, a few weeks ago, shouted "Viva Mussolini!" See him die, and then hear him as I heard him once in the Piazza in the city of Rome stand and shout to the world, "We will crush every sniveling democracy on earth!" And a world shivered. I didn't! Come to the Wilhelmstrasse in the city of Berlin and, down among the twisted steel and mortar, see—crawling upon his belly like the viper he was, his nostrils filled with the stench of his own frying flesh—see Hitler die. And then hear him as I heard him once in the same Wilhelmstrasse say to the world, "The next thousand years belong to Nazism!" Khrushchev, beware! All of history is against you! Americans, be of good courage!

I Believe

One of the most common phrases upon our lips is "I believe." I believe this about some person; I believe this about the international situation; I believe this about our local and domestic problems. I do not propose in this sermon to confine myself to areas that are all too obvious. Rather, I want to give a broad pattern of my own belief about what I consider the fundamental and not the nonessential.

I don't like the word *old* and never use it if I can avoid it. I much prefer the word *mature*. I am not growing old; I am just trying to mature. And if I have about twenty more years of it, I may get some sense along the way. But I am not interested in age merely as a reality which we know is inevitable. There is nothing you can do about your birthday—that's your date—and you can do nothing about the passing years.

Now, one of two things happens when you mature and get older. You become old enough that you may be compelled by experience and history to do some rethinking about the things you have believed and the loyalties you have evidenced. You will be surprised how many things history and experience will compel you to eliminate, things that you can no longer cherish as part of your life, which in the early years might have been the supreme things in your life. Nothing but age, history, and experience will do that. You discard many of your old ideas, for you believe they are no longer practical in your intellectual serenity or in your spiritual achievement. You do not believe them; you do not accept them. They are not a part of your life anymore. It takes maturity to do that; youth cannot do that because the experience and history are not there.

So far I have only stated the negative side; but there's a positive side. History and experience may validate your beliefs. And instead of being compelled to discard some cherished, childhood belief, these beliefs may be confirmed in your mind and experience. You may live long enough either to find the necessity of repudiation of your former beliefs or the verification of them. That is exactly where I am today. I have lived long enough to find verification of things I have believed all my life, both during my youth and during the maturity of these later years.

Now, don't let that experience ever make you a bigot and close your mind, for a closed mind is never a growing mind. When a person shuts the doors of his mind to the infiltration of new scientific, esthetic, or creative truth, he is finished. Always keep the mind open. But when you come to the point where you have validated some of the things you have believed all along the way, then you are progressing.

Now, there are three things that have been a part of my life from the very beginning.

First, I can't remember when I didn't believe the first great reality—that God created man. I have never doubted that. I have never doubted for one minute that the great creative impulse of the cosmos is seen in the variations of the stars and the planets. And all that has happened in science, music, art and literature indicates plainly to me a verification of something I have always believed: that man was created for a great purpose; that human life is about something; that we are something more than biological accidents. Of course we didn't pick our color or parents; we have nothing to do with our origin. I had to begin life with what was handed to me, and so did you. But I believe, as a part of what theology I possess, that the creative intelligence of the cosmos, which I call God, the God of continuing spiritual vitality and creativeness, created man and created him for a purpose. The face of every flower, the laughter of a little child, and the sacrificial fight that I see people making every day of their lives tells me that we are more than machines and more than computers. There is a fundamental relationship between us and the eternal spirit of creativeness. I can't find any better word than *God* for that.

I am not speaking of an anthropomorphic conception of a God that sits in the sky with a long beard and a long spear, which is a creation of the mind of man. I am not discussing God in the narrow, bigoted, sectarian sense—a God that can be defined and

I Believe

measured. Neither you nor I ever read a definition of God that was sufficiently inclusive to incorporate the whole reality of God. If you can define God, you have a limited God who is no God at all. So there are no definitions of God. God has to be an experience, not a definition. The spirit of creativeness, which is a part of the human personality, is a part of God. That's God. And it is that spirit which spurs man onward to something high and lofty. I would ask for no greater evidence of God than that man sooner or later turns toward the sky; that there is an upward enticement in the very constituency of man.

Every generation that has come in world culture has contained a latent dream. Some creative soul, some poet, preached comity and peace. That impulse was never missing from the human heart or human consciousness. To me, that's God operating in humanity. I don't need any creed, ecclesiastical splendor, or sophomoric thinking to verify God. I don't need any verse to describe God in terms of a creed or church. There is an association with the eternal spirit of creativeness, and that's the manifestation of God. Now I believe and have always believed that God created man.

Second, I have never ceased believing that God created man for a great purpose. You just being you is purpose. I have been given identity as Preston Bradley in the humanity of personality. To me—and I have said it repeatedly from this pulpit and repeat it without apology—there are no unimportant people. I don't know any unimportant people. Every person I know is important in the little area and circumference of his own life. Life is important for them: rich or poor, illiterate or learned. They will fight for that life to keep it. Every individual is an important, living soul. I have never doubted that for a moment.

Last, I believe, and have always believed, that God gave man the potential for carrying out the purpose for which he was created. I remember being stricken to the depths at the tragedy and collapse of someone in our little village. I will never forget the horror I felt as a little boy when skating in the old rink one evening during a roller-skating party. I found a drunk man under the floor of the skating rink, wallowing in filth. I looked at that man, I woke him up, and I helped him home. Something settled in my heart—the tragedy of a wasted life.

Life is about something. Not only do I believe that God created man, but I believe God created him for a great purpose. If man has always fought and always will, if the heat and the heartache of American youth struggling in muddy Vietnam is inevitable, and if America cannot rise in the dignity of great leadership, then it would be a tragedy that any of us were born. Why be created if man is caught and trapped by the circle of history and can never achieve the beauty of peace and brotherhood? Man has the potential. How long it will take him I do not know. But God created man; He created him for a great purpose; and He gave man the potential for carrying out that purpose.

Let us, you and I, waste no time or energy in the nonessentials of life, but bend our time and energies toward the highest purposes for which we were God-created.

If I Had Only One Sermon to Preach

If I had only one sermon to preach! Perhaps I have! Life is a very uncertain thing in these hectic and confusing days; and if I had only one sermon to preach, what would that sermon be? That's a sobering thought. Obviously one of these days there will be a last sermon. This equation of life, birth and death, is firmly established; and if we are realistic, we will anticipate the change in the circumstances of life. Really I have never had but one sermon. I have preached only one sermon throughout my entire ministry. I have been dominated by one theme, and every sermon has been only a variation of that theme. And I have put something of that theme into every sermon and every address which I have ever made. So really I have had only one sermon.

If there should be at times evidences of repetition, for that I do not apologize. You go to see *Hamlet,* don't you? You know the whole play, but you go to see it again and again. You know how it is going to end. You know the great speech of Hamlet's soliloquy: "To be, or not to be: that is the question." You know that, but you go to see *Hamlet* at every opportunity. You have heard Chopin's "Nocturne" again and again; but you don't say, "I have heard it before." You return to see a great painting. The Mona Lisa has commanded the admiration of the portrait artists of the earth in their attempt to find the revelation of her soul in that enigmatic smile. You stand before a Monet or a Constable. Thousands of people crowd the art galleries of the world capitals to see a great work of art.

Every creative personality is dominated by one theme. There is a major theme in every life. If I could talk with you intimately and personally for ten minutes, I would discover the dominating theme of your life. I would portray what makes you you. For that dominating theme is continuous in your life, and everything you do is but a variation of that dominating theme.

You come with me to a little old English cottage, where, under the thatched roof, is an old worn case. We open its creaking hinges, and we hold in our hands a manuscript. We do not know who wrote it—the name is not on it—but we read it. And something of the genius of Hamlet, Macbeth, and Iago shines forth, and immediately we say, "No one could write that but Shakespeare. We have found an old portfolio of Shakespeare's, brought to light for the first time." And we can identify it because of the dominating motif of Shakespeare; for there was a motif in Shakespeare whether he was writing comedy, drama, or tragedy. Whatever he wrote, there was a touch of the dramatist-genius Shakespeare.

Come with me to the coast of Normandy. See there a little old French cottage and examine an old cabinet. In it you find a canvas. You unroll it, and you see figures. No name is signed to it, but you have seen that before. It is *The Angelus,* the reapers. You have no trouble identifying the picture. No one but Millet could have painted it, and you know it. Every life has a dominating theme.

What is the dominating imperative of your life? Are you sure that you know what it is? If you discover that, you will find the answer for living life. Every great artist, poet, dramatist, and creative personality has a great imperative. I do not pretend to classify myself in the ranks of the geniuses, but I do put myself in the category of being dominated by a great motif. I have put something of that domination in every sermon I have preached, every lecture I have given, and every book I have written. You will discover it there. The dominating motif of my life has colored all my thinking, all my actions.

Influenced and conditioned by a deep fundamental understanding of the integrity of one's mind, I have never surrendered the right of individual thinking. I have never permitted a creed, ceremony, organization, or party to be substituted for my own right of thinking for myself. I have thought for myself in theology; I have thought for myself politically; I have thought for myself in the creative arts. Thinking for oneself frequently puts one in the minority, but I have never been interested in being in the majority. I have never been interested in being on the side of the greatest power and the greatest force. I have tried to avoid the mistake that so many have made in thinking that greatness and bigness are the same thing. I have never had any mental clog in my mind that being big is being great, or that being great is necessarily being big. Greatness and bigness are not similar; and yet a great many people in religion, philosophy, and politics are constantly confused by thinking that if a thing is big then it is the most powerful and the strongest. The greatest influences on earth are the silent ones and the unseen ones. You never saw love. All you ever saw was the result of love; but love itself you never saw. You never saw the wind; no one yet ever saw the wind. The only thing you saw was the result of the wind—the tornado; but you didn't see the wind. The greatest influences of life are the silent ones.

Now, what is the dominating motif that I have tried through the years to put in every sermon? I think most of you could probably give the next two or three sentences for me. I want it to be said of me after I am gone and the last sermon has been preached and the last experience of life has been lived—I would rather have written upon any remnant that I leave, this sentence than any other: "He tried to be a friend of all mankind." I would rather have that said of me than to have written the best book of my generation, than to have preached the greatest sermon. I would rather have it said of me than to command great wealth or great power: "He was a friend of man." That's my motivation.

One of the things that gives me great compensation in these twilight years is the fact that I have respected and honored the dignity of the personality, whether it was covered with a black skin or a yellow, a white or a brown. And it matters less and less to me all the time. For I happen to believe that, deep down underneath all these superficial distinctions that are the result of environment and of history, before a person is a Negro, before he is white or brown or yellow, he is first a human being. That's first. That's before your color; that's before anything else in your life. You are a human being, and as a human being you are amenable to all the principles and forces and influences that affect humanity. In a world bewitched by racial hatreds, by religious bigotries, by misunderstandings, by the fury of little people, by the consideration of the unimportant and the dignifying of the nonessential, underneath it all is a human heart. And if we could begin all of our struggles about politics, international relations, poverty, and racial conflicts on the basis of our common humanity, I tremble to think what the results would be.

It would be the beginning of the Kingdom on earth, which our Master once asked us to build. And our mission is to build the Kingdom of God—where? On the moon? He never mentioned that. Where to build it? On the earth! Here, where we live, in the environment that our lungs are built for. My lungs were built for the oxygen of earth; my body was built for the earth, and so was yours. And if we could begin this great pilgrimage for humanity with our common humanity, it makes me almost breathless to think about what would happen.

So the one sermon, the first one and the last one: love. For love remains the mighty potential and the quivering vibrant theme that would translate hell into heaven and create a paradise on this earth. That has been the theme of my life: to love humanity, mankind. It shall continue to be until the last breath.

NOTES

1 Preston Bradley, *Courage for Today* (Indianapolis and New York: The Bobbs-Merrill Company, 1934), pp. 68-69.
2 Bradley, "The Atheist Nobody Knows," *The Liberal*, IV (December, 1927), p. 8.
3 Bradley, *Mastering Fear* (Indianapolis and New York: The Bobbs-Merrill Company, 1935), p. 35.
4 Bradley, *Along the Way* (New York: David McKay, 1962), p. 42.
5 Bradley, "The Atheist Nobody Knows," pp. 7-8.
6 Bradley, "Forty-five Years of Preaching," *The Liberalist*, XXXIV (April, 1957), p. 15.
7 *Ibid.*, pp. 11, 14-18.
8 Bradley, *Along the Way*, p. 41.
9 Bradley, *Life and You* (New York and London: Harper and Brothers, 1939), p. 30.
10 Bradley, *Along the Way*, p. 38.
11 Bradley, "The Living Shakespeare," *The Liberalist*, XVI (May, 1939), pp. 8-9.
12. "After 53 Years in Ministry, Dr. Bradley Is Still Full of Bounce," *Chicago's American*, November 8, 1964, section I, p. 18.
13 Bradley, "Forty-five Years of Preaching," p. 15.
14 Bradley, *Along the Way*, p. 57.
15 *Ibid.*, p. 59.
16 Bradley, *Courage for Today*, p. 50.
17 Bradley, *Along the Way*, p. 56.
18 *Ibid.*, p. 256.
19 Bradley, "The Atheist Nobody Knows," pp. 10-11.
20 Bradley, "Where Is God Now?" *The Liberalist*, XVIII (February, 1942), p. 12.
21 Bradley, *Along the Way*, p. 79.
22 Bradley, "Courage," *The Liberalist*, XXXIX (January, 1963), p. 11.
23 Bradley, *Along the Way*, p. 111.
24 Bradley, "The Future of the Peoples Church," *The Liberal*, III (September, 1926), p. 3.

25 "Pastor's Pace," *Newsweek,* October 1, 1962, pp. 59-60.

26 Bradley, *Along the Way,* p. 116.

27 Connie Meyers, "55 Years of Service to His City," *Chicago's American,* October 15, 1967, section 3, p. 10.

28 Bradley, "The Future of the Peoples Church," p. 3.

29 *Fiftieth Golden Anniversary* (Chicago: The Peoples Church of Chicago, 1962), p. 8.

30 "Freeport Chautauqua Assembly," program-pamphlet for the Freeport, Ohio, Chautauqua meeting, August 12-20, 1911, p. 5.

31 "Bradley Too Orthodox," *The Lyceum Magazine,* December, 1915, p. 47.

32 "Dr. Bradley a 'Whirlwind,'" *The Lyceum News,* March-April, 1920, p. 3.

33 Gilbert Frankau, *My Unsentimental Journey* (London: Hutchinson and Company, n.d.), first edition, p. 121.

34 Leonard Dubkin, "Dr. Bradley's Retirement Signals End of Era Here," *Lerner Newspapers,* Week of June 18, 1968, p. 1.

35 Bradley, "What Is a Liberal?" *The Liberal,* I (April, 1924), p. 3.

36 Bradley, *Along the Way,* p. 125.

37 "Breaking of Ground Service," *The Liberal,* II (July, 1925), pp. 5-8.

38 Orvin Larson, *American Infidel: Robert G. Ingersoll* (New York: Citadel Press, 1962). Also Wayland Maxfield Parrish and Alfred Dwight Houston, "Robert G. Ingersoll," *A History and Criticism of American Public Address,* ed. by William Norwood Brigance, I (New York: McGraw Hill, 1943), pp. 363-386.

39 Allen Johnson and Dumas Malone, eds., "Robert Collyer," *Dictionary of American Biography,* IV (New York: Charles Scribner's Sons, 1930), pp. 310-311. Also John Haynew Holmes, *The Life and Letters of Robert Collyer, 1823-1912* (New York: Dodd, Mead and Company, 1917).

40 Bradley, "The Spirit of Religious Freedom," *The Liberal,* II (September, 1925), pp. 6-12.

41 Robert Collyer, *Some Memoirs* (Boston: American Unitarian Association, 1908), pp. 235-236.

42 Harry M. Williams, "David Swing: The Voice of Music Hall," *Speech Monographs,* XV (1948), pp. 44-60. Also Joseph Fort Newton, *David Swing—Poet Preacher* (Chicago: Unity Publishing Company, 1909).

43 Almer M. Pennewell, *The Methodist Movement in Northern Illinois* (Sycamore, Illinois: The Sycamore Tribune, 1942), pp. 50-51.

44 *Fiftieth Golden Anniversary,* p. 6.

45 "After 53 Years in Ministry, Dr. Bradley Is Still Full of Bounce," p. 18.

Notes

46 Bradley, "Editorial, a Tribute to Grace Thayer Bradley, My Wife," *The Liberalist,* XXVII (July, 1950), pp. 17-18.
47 Bradley, "Grace Thayer Bradley, a Biographical Sketch," *The Liberalist,* XXVII (July, 1950), pp. 9-10.
48 Bradley, "The Future of The Peoples Church," pp. 3-4.
49 Bradley, "The Dedication of Our Church," *The Liberal,* III (October, 1926), p. 4.
50 Ralph Schoenleben, "Prodigious Preston Bradley," *The Liberalist,* XIX (September, 1942), p. 16.
51 Bradley, "The Dedication of Our Church," pp. 3-4.
52 Bradley, "Modern Life and the Church," *The Liberal,* III (October, 1926), p. 8.
53 Bradley, "My Religion," *The Liberal,* XIII (June, 1936), p. 10.
54 Bradley, "If," *The Liberalist,* XXXVIII (August, 1961), pp. 15-16.
55 Bradley, "A Sunday in the Old Home Church," *The Liberal,* I (October, 1924), p. 5.
56 Bradley, "What Is the Peoples Church?" *The Liberalist,* XXXVI (July, 1959), p. 9.
57 Bradley, "What Is the Peoples Church of Chicago?" *The Liberalist,* XIX (April, 1942), pp. 31, 33.
58 William F. M'Dermott, "One Busy Man, the Story of Peoples Church," *Chicago Daily News,* March 21, 1942, p. 3.
59 John H. Sengstacke, "Dr. Preston Bradley," *Chicago Defender,* September 18, 1962, p. 12.
60 Louis Mann, quoted, *The Liberalist,* XIV (June, 1937), p. 15.
61 "The First Church of Preston Bradley," *American Magazine,* April, 1943, p. 128.
62 Charles Clayton Morrison, "Dr. Preston Bradley," *The Liberalist,* XXXI (July, 1954), p. 8.
63 Earle Harvey, "Chicago Firsts: Dr. Preston Bradley," *Chicago's American,* April 1, 1957, p. 13.
64 Bradley, "Some Radio Experiences," *The Liberalist,* XIV (September, 1937), p. 9.
65 "Fete to Honor Dr. Bradley," *Chicago's American,* March 24, 1957, p. 29.
66 "Kup's Column," *Chicago Sun-Times,* October 1, 1953, p. 46.
67 Dale Harrison, "All About the Town," *Chicago Sun,* March 14, 1945, section II, p. 15.
68 Bradley, "Along the Way," *The Liberalist,* XL (May, 1963), p. 6.
69 Bradley, "Along the Way," *The Liberalist,* XXIX (February, 1963), p. 6.
70 Bradley, "Along the Way," *The Liberalist,* XLI (March, 1964), p. 7.
71 *Ibid.,* p. 6.
72 Bradley, "Some Radio Experiences," p. 13.

73 *Ibid.,* p. 14.

74 Bradley, "Meaning of the Pope's Visit," *The Liberalist,* XLII (November, 1965), p. 7.

75 Bradley, "What's the Use?" *The Liberalist,* XXXIX (April, 1962), p. 16.

76 Bradley, "In Deep Waters," *The Liberalist,* XL (October, 1963), p. 14.

77 Citation from the Chicago Chapter, the Friends of Literature, to Dr. Preston Bradley, May 9, 1942.

78 M'Dermott, "The Peoples Church Will Honor Pastor-Founder Tomorrow," *Chicago Daily News,* June 8, 1940, p. 13.

79 Dorothy Dockstader, "Lecture-goers Read Books," *The Publishers' Weekly,* June 2, 1934, p. 2063.

80 Grace Thayer Bradley, "The Twenty-fifth Anniversary," *The Liberalist,* XV (July, 1938), pp. 5-6.

81 G. T. Bradley, "Dr. Bradley Is Honored," *The Liberalist,* XV (July, 1938), pp. 5-6.

82 G. T. Bradley, "Doctor Bradley Receives Degree," *The Liberalist,* XVI (August, 1939), pp. 5-6.

83 G. T. Bradley, "Dr. Bradley Adopted by Chippewas," *The Liberalist,* XVII (September, 1940), 13-15.

84 Schoenleben, "Prodigious Preston Bradley," pp. 15-16.

85 *Ibid.,* p. 17.

86 Herb Graffis, "May You Always Keep Looking Up," *Award 55,* Program for the civic dinner honoring Dr. Preston Bradley, October 20, 1967, p. 9.

87 Earl Nightingale, in the Foreword to Dr. Preston Bradley's *Happiness Through Creative Living* (Garden City, New York: Hanover House, 1955), p. 7.

88 *Newsweek,* April 8, 1957, p. 68.

89 *Mesabi Daily News,* quoted in *The Liberalist,* XLI (October, 1964), p. 19.

90 Meyers, "55 Years of Service to His City," p. 10.

91 Carl I. Henrikson, "A Tribute to Dr. Bradley," *The Liberalist,* XXXII (August, 1955), p. 8.

92 *Time,* April 26, 1937, p. 29.

93 Schoenleben, "Prodigious Preston Bradley," p. 17.

94 *Newsweek,* April 8, 1957, p. 69.

95 *Newsweek,* October 1, 1962, p. 59.

96 M'Dermott, "The Peoples Church Will Honor Pastor-Founder Tomorrow," p. 13.

97 M'Dermott, "One Busy Man, the Story of Peoples Church," p. 3.

98 *American Magazine,* April, 1943, p. 128.

99 "Dr. Bradley Marks 35 Years as Pastor," *Chicago Sunday Times,* April 20, 1947, p. 29.
100 Adele Hoskins, "Highest Paid Air Clergyman—It's Chicago's Dr. Bradley," *Chicago Daily News,* June 8, 1946, p. 23.
101 Delores McCahill, "Dr. Bradley Sets Sermon Marking 50 Years as Pastor," *Chicago Sun-Times,* April 28, 1962, p. 18.
102 Herb Graffis, "The Friendly Literates," *Chicago Sun-Times,* April 28, 1956, p. 18.
103 *Newsweek,* October 1, 1962, pp. 59-60.
104 Dave Meade, "46 Years a Preacher Here and Still Going," *Chicago Daily News,* August 16, 1958, p. 10.
105 Stanley Pieza, "Dr. Bradley Pastor 50 Years," *Chicago's American,* April 28, 1962, p. 11.
106 Bradley, *Along the Way,* pp. 40-41.
107 "Modernism to Win, Says Preston Bradley," *Herald and Examiner,* May 3, 1925, p. 2.
108 "Pastor Fights Draft," *Chicago Sun,* March 5, 1945, p. 7.
109 "Bradley Assails Officer's Order Curbing Worship," *Chicago Daily Tribune,* November 10, 1941, p. 8.
110 "G. L. K. Smith Hall Rental Put Up to Union," *Chicago Sun,* March 13, 1945, section II, p. 13.
111 "3 Pastors Ask Ike to Spare Spies," *Chicago's American,* June 15, 1953, p. 6.
112 "Sbarbaro, Bradley Plead for Leopold," *Chicago's American,* April 24, 1957, p. 7.
113 "Bradley Favors Nazi Trials," *Chicago Sun-Times,* January 18, 1965, p. 14.
114 "Dr. Preston Bradley Rejects Bid to Run for Congress," *Chicago Daily News,* July 19, 1962, p. 26.
115 Marjorie Dent Candec, ed., *Current Biography 1956* (New York: H. W. Wilson Company, 1956), p. 74.
116 "Kup's Column," *Chicago Sun-Times,* October 18, 1953, p. 44.
117 U. S. Congress, House, Preston Bradley delivering prayer, 87th Congress, 2nd session, September 28, 1962, *Congressional Record,* CVIII, p. 21149.
118 Bradley, "Life's Deeper Meanings," *The Liberalist,* XXXIX (November, 1962), p. 14.
119 Bradley, "Red or Dead," sermon preached at the Peoples Church of Chicago, October 22, 1961, p. 1.
120 Bradley, "Forty-five Years of Preaching," p. 17.
121 *Ibid.,* p. 18.
122 Citation, Board of Trustees of Yankton College, *The Liberalist,* XLIII (August, 1966), p. 3.

123 "Dinner To Mark Dr. Bradley's Term," *Sun-Times,* March 23, 1957, p. 12.

124 Walter F. Morse, "A Preacher's Personal Tale," *Chicago Sun-Times,* September 23, 1962, section III, p. 2.

125 "After 53 Years in Ministry, Dr. Bradley Is Still Full of Bounce," p. 18.

126 "Dr. Bradley Adds Church Affiliation," *Chicago Sun-Times* January 13, 1956, p. 5.

127 Letter from Adlai E. Stevenson, Libertyville, Illinois, January 18, 1956.

128 Ethel Wells Smalley, "Dedication of the Preston Bradley Chapel in the Peoples Church," *The Liberalist,* XLI (May, 1964), pp. 12-13.

129 Smalley, "Reflections From the Pastor's Study," *The Liberalist,* XLI (May, 1964), p. 14.

130 Bradley, "Chapel," *The Liberalist,* XLI (May, 1964), p. 10.

131 Pieza, "Dr. Bradley Hailed as Preacher-Teacher," *Chicago's American,* September 22, 1962, p. 4.

132 Otto Kerner, quoted, "Dr. Bradley Is Honored by 500 at Dinner," *Chicago Tribune,* September 22, 1962, part one, p. 14.

133 Bradley, quoted by Sarah Boyden, "A Firm Faith in the Future," *Midwest Magazine, Chicago Sunday Sun-Times,* November 19, 1961, p. 20.

134 Meyers, "55 Years of Service to His City," *Chicago's American,* October 15, 1967, section III, p. 10.

135 Everett Dirksen, quoted, *Award 55,* Program celebration, October 20, 1967, p. 12.

136 Proclamation by Governor Kerner, Springfield, Illinois, September 19, 1967.

137 Proclamation by Mayor Daley, Chicago, Illinois, September 13, 1967.

138 Bradley, "Forty-five Years of Preaching," p. 11.

139 Bradley, *Life and You,* pp. 12-13.

140 Bradley, "Forty-five Years of Preaching," p. 17.

141 Bradley, "In Deep Waters," p. 15.

142 Harry Barnard, in "A Note by the Collaborator," from Dr. Preston Bradley's *Along the Way,* p. 280.

143 "After 53 Years in Ministry, Dr. Bradley Is Still Full of Bounce," p. 18.

144 Morrison, "Dr. Preston Bradley," p. 7.

145 Bradley, "Emerson's Influence on Modern Thought," *The Liberalist,* X (July, 1933), p. 11.

146 Bradley, "Mothers Around the World," *The Liberalist,* XLII (June, 1965), pp. 7-8.

147 Bradley, "If I Had Only One Sermon To Preach," *The Liberalist,* XLII (March, 1966), p. 17.

148 "After 53 Years in Ministry, Dr. Bradley Is Still Full of Bounce," p. 18.

149 "Festival to Mark the Birthday of Gautama Buddha," *Chicago Sun-Times,* April 4, 1964, p. 14.

150 Bradley, "Along the Way," *The Liberalist,* XLI (May, 1964), p. 5.

151 Bradley, "Along the Way," *The Liberalist,* XL (July, 1963), p. 8.

152 G. T. Bradley, "Arden," *The Liberal,* I (July, 1924), p. 5.

153 Smalley, "A Soliloquy," *The Liberalist,* XX (September, 1943), p. 18.

154 G. T. Bradley, "Evening," *The Liberal,* II (August, 1925), p. 16.

155 G. T. Bradley, "An Autumn Reverie," *The Liberal,* I (September, 1924), p. 11.

156 G. T. Bradley, "Shadows," *The Liberal,* II (September, 1925), p. 13.

157 Bradley, "Along the Way," *The Liberalist,* XLI (September, 1964), p. 5.

BIBLIOGRAPHY

BOOKS

Bradley, Preston. *Along the Way.* New York: David McKay, 1962.
———. *Between You and Me.* Chicago: Aspley House, 1967.
———. *Courage for Today.* Indianapolis and New York: Bobbs-Merrill, 1934.
———. *Happiness Through Creative Living.* Garden City: Hanover House, 1955.
———. *Life and You.* New York and London: Harper and Brothers, 1939.
———. *Mastering Fear.* Indianapolis and New York: Bobbs-Merrill, 1935.
———. *Meditations.* Chicago: The Peoples Church of Chicago, 1941; Chicago: Wilcox and Follett, 1946.
———. *Meditations and My Daily Strength.* New York: Permabooks, 1946.
———. *My Daily Strength.* Chicago: Wilcox and Follett, 1943.
———. *New Wealth for You.* New York: Frederick A. Stokes Co., 1941.
———. *Power From Right Thinking.* Indianapolis and New York: Bobbs-Merrill, 1936.

MANUSCRIPTS AND CLIPPINGS

Bradley, Preston, mss. In his study, 2608 Lake View Drive, Chicago. This assortment contains his correspondence, photographs, scrapbooks, church files, unpublished sermons, tape-recorded speeches and sermons, bound copies of the church magazine, and his journal.
Bradley, Preston, mss. Special Collections, the University of Illinois at Chicago Circle. This official collection constitutes the primary deposit of Preston Bradley materials.
Clipping file of *Chicago's American.* This specialized newspaper file contains numerous clippings on Preston Bradley.
Clipping file of *Chicago Sun-Times.* This specialized file contains numerous clippings on Preston Bradley.